I0169494

A Philosopher
Looks

at
The Sense
of
Humor

Richard C. Richards

Copyright Notice

Copyright © 2013 Richard C. Richards

A Philosopher Looks at The Sense of Humor

Published by Healing Time Books
First Print Edition: July 2013
First Digital Edition: July 2013
Digital Download available for Kindle, iPad, Nook and other e-readers (Kindle eBooks - www.amazon.com) and mobile devices (iPhone and Android)

Website: www.philosopherlooksathumor.com

All Rights Reserved.
No part of this book may be reproduced by any mechanical, photographic or electronic process, or in the form of a phonographic recording; nor may it be stored in a retrieval system, transmitted, or otherwise to be copied for public or private use - other than for "fair use" as brief quotations embodied in articles and reviews without prior written permission of the publisher.

Royalty-free images licensed through Getty Images:
  Cover Image Copyright Bluem00ner
  Title Page Image Copyright Floridapfe from S. Korea Kim in Cherl

Library of Congress Control Number: 2013942297
Philosophy : Wit : Humor : Laughter : Aesthetics : Comedy

ISBN-13: 978-0-9821052-5-2
ISBN-10: 0-9821052-5-8

Print Edition available through Amazon's CreateSpace.com
eStore at https://www.createspace.com/4323079

Digital Edition in Kindle format available through Amazon.com

Healing Time Books
www.healingtimebooks.com

Dedication

For

Marlene

"Marty"

An

Extraordinary

Woman

A Philosopher Looks at The Sense of Humor

Contents

Chapter 9 *continued*
Yet Another Question: How to Settle These Issues.
A Significant Question: Good Taste. Jokes and Humor.
Why Not Another Question: Commonality of the Sense of Humor. Who are the Humorists? So You're a Damned Elitist, Aren't You?
Conclusion.

"Education is an admirable thing, but it is well to remember from time to time that nothing that is worth knowing can be taught."

Oscar Wilde

"Most people think they have a great sense of humor. They also think they are great lovers, which pretty much proves that they have a great sense of humor."

Richard C. Richards

"Only write for those who can read between the lines."

Richard "Kinky" Friedman

Forward

I don't want to be too forward, but I can hear you ask yourself, deep down where you ask important questions, "Why another book on humor?" Especially since this book does not contain any humor. The answer is simple. This book is not about humor, but about what a sense of humor is. That's different. That's important.

So, "Forward March."

The importance of dealing with the nature of a sense of humor can be best understood if we compare humor to love. Many people have asked the question, "What is love?" especially after some promising relationship has taken a nose dive into the swamp of life. It is, however, misleading to ask such a question about a general noun such as "love." There is actually no such thing as love, but only loving actions, loving people, and loving relationships. It is better to ask "What is loving?" or "What is the ability to love?" since loving is a process carried on by living, conscious beings. It's simply clearer to avoid seeking a definition for a general noun like "love," though fairly satisfactory definitions can be given. These definitions are by their very nature somewhat misleading.

It is the same with the question of humor. To ask "What is humor?" tends to send the investigation in the wrong direction, as if there were some object called humor to find, much like an intrepid explorer looking for an endangered species. The more rewarding investigation should be framed in terms of a sense of humor, which is a characteristic shown mostly by human beings. Or at least many human beings.

I will nevertheless do some work on the concept of humor because it has a long and somewhat respectable past, but seeking the nature of the sense of humor is much more enlightening. Seeking an understanding of humor is a good first step, as long as we are aware of the pitfalls.

Everyone is supposed to love a person with a sense of humor. Every person knows for sure they have a good sense of humor, and it is one of their more positive assets. They also desire it in other people. Consider all the personal descriptions people create when they are looking for relationships with other people. Besides such relatively trivial qualities as youth, good looks, a small fortune, and no encumbrances such as a spouse or two, people almost always mention that they are seeking a person with a good sense of humor. You know, someone who can laugh at the handicapped, chortle in victory in trivial games involving no skill at all, cackle while they torture small mammals—you know, wonderful people. Just like you and me. Or at least like the neighbors.

In obituaries, one of the things mentioned about the dearly departed is that they had a sense of humor. One wonders whether they will need it now. Since we all admire a sense of humor, maybe we should stop to consider what it is.

This will of course involve to some extent stating what humor is, which is somewhat important if we are going to have a sense of it. We're going to have to define a few terms, such as "humor," "comedy," "play," "fun," and related terms. That will be no fun at all. In fact, understanding these things is dreadful, dreary work, but the sense of satisfaction gained by understanding these issues will in no possible way compensate for the intense agony required to reach that understanding. You need to know this now.

This just happens to be the way life is, but that realization is of little value during the suffering. As the French say, usually in French, "C'est la vie," which roughly translates as "Get over it." This is good advice for most everything in life, including life itself. Sooner or later we will have to get over it, whether we want to or not. After all, death is something one does not easily live through.

It doesn't help at all to understand these things, but it can be enough to justify a book anyway.

As a humane gesture more than as a public service, I will summarize some of my assumptions, goals, and methods to save the reader the trouble of actually reading the rest of the book. Goodness knows that is a dreary enough task, and I haven't read the whole thing myself for that very reason.

One of my theses is that a sense of humor can best be understood by comparing it with a sense of the aesthetic. Since aestheticians have spent considerable time attempting to clarify what a sense of the aesthetic is, indeed enough time to thoroughly confuse the issue, I will ruthlessly exploit the comparison that I believe holds between a sense of humor and a sense of the aesthetic. I will ride that sorry comparison until it collapses under me.

The comparison works well because I believe that in fact, humor is one category in the aesthetic, and the relationship we are pursuing is one of class inclusion. An example of this is the inclusion of the class of dogs in the class of mammals. All dogs are mammals, but not all mammals are dogs. Likewise, all humor belongs in the

3

category of the aesthetic, but there are many aesthetic objects and experiences that are not humorous in the least.

Nevertheless my investigation requires only that we grant there are simply similarities between the aesthetic and the humorous, and I can explore that as an explicative analogy. Pursuing a comparison between the aesthetic and humorous seems to me to be a good way to understand the humorous, and what a sense of humor is. We do not have to accept my additional belief that the humorous is a subclass of the aesthetic, though that assumption offers yet more insights into a sense of humor.

The comparison clarifies the notion of the sense of humor, as long as I carefully control the characterization of the sense of the aesthetic. The proof that the comparison has value will be established by the quality and quantity of the insights it provides into the nature of the sense of humor. Understanding does bring some satisfaction in a world dominated by the triviality of politics, economics, and sitcoms.

My background is in philosophy, whose most important contribution to knowledge is the clarification of concepts. The first distinction I take up in the next chapter is the relationship between laughter and humor. The distinction simply is this: laughter is an example of behavior, and humor is an example of a mental phenomenon. It is that simple, but the simple is often overlooked because it seems so obvious. So obviously it is not that simple.

Some readers may be uncomfortable with the relative paucity of any scholarly citations in the book, while some will be delighted by the near absence. There will be enough to satisfy the ordinary reader, but certainly not enough to satisfy the collector. I don't want to lose the quarry in a jungle of distracting footnotes.

Our friends in the psychological world may feel ignored by the content of this book. It is not that I am unfamiliar with their work. The problem is often that they need to be as empirical as they can, and they often do that by measuring physical phenomena such as the physical behavior of laughter, which may or may not be correlated with any kind of psychological behavior such as the reaction to and the appreciation of humor.

Sometimes psychologists and other theoreticians confuse laughter with humor, and even confuse laughter with comedy or jokes. This renders their studies open to some fundamental methodological criticisms. It also makes them unhelpful for our inquiry, which aims at the production of the highest degree of conceptual clarity. Perhaps this book can be helpful in supplying the degree of conceptual clarity needed to carry on psychological studies involving a sense of humor in a more productive manner.

In our tour of the wide, wonderful world of the humorous, we will touch upon such issues as what causes a sense of humor, whether it can be taught, what its value may be, how it is connected with happiness, and whether it should be placed on the endangered species list. We will of necessity explore the habitat of the amusing, the entertaining, and the comedic. There is considerable laughter in the world, and a more than abundant supply of things to laugh at. But since laughter and humor are only partially and not essentially connected, this may end up being a eulogy for the death of humor. Perhaps this book will cause it. We can only hope.

Pax vobiscum.[1] Rest in pieces, blithe spirit. We hardly knew ye.

Old Aristotle said that we should expect only as much clarity as the subject matter will allow. I hope to come close to that limit. But please take his observation as a caveat.

Needless to say, if you've gotten this far without a nagging realization that something less than serious is occasionally going on in this book, I don't need to warn you that I play and joke almost as much as I'm serious, and that you need to bring a rather large salt shaker with you on this raid on the incomprehensible.

On the other hand, there is enough serious stuff going on to hopefully satisfy the more sober minded among us. Sometimes it is hard to tell which of the two is going on. Sometimes it just might be both, or neither.

Pox vobiscum. This book may be that pox.[2]

Endnotes

[1] Fancy Latin phrase for fancy Latinos.

[2] It has been argued by people who know much more about these things than I do, that you cannot have only a single footnote in a chapter. Or even an introduction. Responding to their expert advice, I have added this footnote to overcome that objection.[3]

[3] Footnotes may be the worst pox of all.[4]

[4] Some will note that I switch between using the phrases "the sense of humor" and "a sense of humor." This is intentional. I use the phrase "the sense of humor" when I am talking about the sense of humor in general. I use the phrase "a sense of humor" when I am referring to individual senses of humor, which vary in detailed ways because of the idiosyncratic nature of human beings. All senses of humor share the essential characteristics of the sense of humor, which is that it is a higher-level abstraction. If you noticed the difference between the two phrases, I'll bet that now you're sorry you did.

"Outside of a dog, a book is man's best friend. Inside of a dog, it's too dark to read."

Groucho Marx

"Ever wonder if illiterate people get the full effect of alphabet soup?"

John Mendoza

"I opened a box of animal crackers, but there was nothing inside. They'd eaten each other."

Lily Tomlin

Chapter 1

Laughter and Humor

The distinction between laughter and humor is so fundamental and crucial that it deserves a whole chapter. I'll state the differences as clearly as I can, and then we can deal with some details and implications. I'll proceed with the issue by characterizing the nouns "laughter" and "humor" since that is simpler than dealing with the "behavior of laughter" and the "experience of humor," which are more accurate descriptions. Later we will deal with the much more complex issues involved with understanding what the sense of humor is.

In the introduction I suggested that the pursuit of definitions for nouns is to be avoided. Generally it is. The present attempt at clarity is a case in which the analysis of nouns should cause no problems that cannot be remedied later. Plus it is a bit clearer and simpler... for a while.

Laughter is an example of physical behavior. Coughing is another example. There is usually some conscious and often reasonable thought process behind the behavior of laughter, but not always and not necessarily. There may be an accompanying emotion or set of emotions, often called "mirth," in the case of humor, but in at least some cases of laughter there is no such emotion or set of emotions. The hollow laughter of the insane is an example of this. The behavior caused by nitrous oxide ("laughing gas") is another. We have all seen the behavior of laughter, and in many cases have probably engaged in it ourselves. You can even do it in pubic if you're careful. Try not to do it when a politician is speaking.

Humor, on the other hand, is an example of a conscious

realization, meaning that it occurs fundamentally on the mental level, occasionally with no overt signs on the level of observable physical behavior. Of course there are always some sort of physiological processes going on in the body at any given time. If you have no physiological processes going on at all, you're in serious trouble. The enjoyment of humor may be accompanied by laughter, but not necessarily. There may simply be a smile, or a nod, or in the case of a particularly bad pun, signs of distress. Signs of distress are perhaps not to be taken too seriously in the case of a pun. Some punsters take it as a compliment. I am not convinced of the truth of this latter point. You can take it or leave it. As Cleopatra said to Caesar, "Julius, I'm not prone to argue."

The enjoyment of humor involves either appreciating it or creating it. I am not going to claim that either one of these activities is better than the other. However, the ability to create humor does give a person more possibilities in life and therefore more power.

The two phenomena, laughter and humor, can occur separately. In other words "laughter" and "humor" are not synonyms. There can be laughter without humor, and there can be humor without laughter, or even without smiling.

The Philosophy of Laughter

This book is mostly about the philosophy of humor, or better, a sense of humor. It is only partially about the philosophy of laughter, but examining laughter is important in understanding the sense of humor. Behavior such as laughter can be observed, the circumstances in which it occurs can be documented, and the possible emotions connected with it can be investigated by questionnaire and introspection, as well as empathetic guessing if need be. Philosophy rarely consists solely of any of these activities, which are more properly the domain of study of the physical and psychological sciences. Philosophy may utilize the findings of the empirical sciences, however, in its speculation. The method pursued by philosophy has sometimes been characterized as the WAG method. WAG is the acronym for Wild-Assed Guess. There is some truth in this observation. Governmental and many other organizations have perfected the WAG method. This may be one of the reasons they are potentially so laughable.

One of the things philosophy can do, with regard to a philosophy of laughter, is to attempt to define laughter, which is a conceptual enterprise, and then attempt to deal with the problems. For example, since laughter is behavior, what kind of behavior will constitute laughter? Will smiling, grinning, chuckling, wheezing, snickering, and other observable bits of behavior be included? A clear stipulative definition will attempt to settle these questions. Will forced laughter, fake laughter, stage laughter, or a "horse laugh" be included, with or without the actual horse? Who said the job would be easy?[1]

I won't define laughter. But I have just attempted to indicate what some of the problems are that must be faced by those attempting such a definition. Laughter, like pornography, may not be easily definable, but most of us know the real thing when we encounter it.

Laughter may be a sign that a person has a sense of humor, but it is not a reliable sign. People can enjoy and even initiate humor without a sign of visible laughter. Indeed a straight face is one of the devices some comedians and humorists have used to set up their comedy or humor. On the other hand, many people laugh when nothing close to humor is involved. A person laughing at the suffering of others is an example. Shades of *"America's Funniest Home Videos."*

The study of overt behavior doesn't require too much of philosophy's tools beyond that of definitional clarity. Once past that, most examples of the philosophy of laughter seem to be attempts to discover what makes people laugh, or in what circumstances we laugh, and that is more properly an empirical investigation, at least initially, until some more terminological problems come up. Then enter the philosopher, stage right, laughing all the way.

Philosophy proceeds through the careful use of language, with very little observation of behavior, and it is not the behavior that is the primary focus. The techniques of philosophy can be applied to laughter, but the behavior involved with humor is mostly mental, much more complex, and is not the direct object of empirical investigation, as it would be in the case of a study of the behavior of laughter. Philosophy is in part engaged in the process of understanding the terminology and assumptions involved in talking about humor. That process is judged in part by how well it explains our experience.

An Empirical Study of Laughter

There has been insufficient empirical inquiry into the behavior of laughter, common as it may be. There has been some speculation about laughter historically, and some assumptions have been made, but only a relatively small amount of systematic empirical study exists, and these tend to be fragmented and partial. Fortunately that situation has been mostly corrected by the recent publication of a book by Robert Provine, called appropriately enough

Laughter: A Scientific Investigation.[2] His approach is to simply observe laughter, or more precisely, who laughs at what, when, and where. Such an approach is more likely to yield data rather than theories, and the data of empirical observation are precisely what we need here for the foundations of our philosophical inquiry.

Provine's conclusions may be surprising to many people. I'll summarize some of his conclusions here, and save you the trouble of reading a well-written, well-supported, and thoughtful book. That does not absolve you of the responsibility to buy the book anyway. We need to support the publication of good books, and the book will look great on your library shelf. Leave it open somewhere in your home to impress people. Put it next to this book and make an even more spectacular impression.

Provine finds that most human laughter occurs in social situations, often as a form of "social lubricant." Joke-telling and stand-up comedy are minor sources of laughter, and atypical. Laughter in social situations is rarely accompanied by anything remotely humorous or funny. Laughter is under weak conscious control of the laugher at best. It is behavior that has apparently served the human race and our primate ancestors for millennia, seems to have become part of our non-conscious behavior in most cases, and follows recognizable patterns. Behavior of this sort usually persists because it has become part of our "hard wiring." Usually this indicates the survival value of the behavior. While there is some speculation in his book, Provine usually labels that speculation as theory or hypothesis, as is appropriate for a physical scientist or anyone attempting to think clearly.

Provine suggests we can learn a bit about laughter from our primate friends, mostly the chimps, and to a lesser extent the gorillas and the orangutans. Chimps have been studied more extensively since they have the strongest union. All of these primates mentioned do laugh, but it is not recognized as laughter by most people, who misidentify it as panting. Chimps can utter only one sound per breath for physiological reasons, which makes any verbal assertion on their part rather simple. Nevertheless the human laugh structure is there in the chimps, and experts in primate behavior verify that much chimp "panting" is their version of laughter. It is most often elicited in chimps by tickling, rough and tumble play, or chasing games, all of which are social events. Chimp laughter can be an invitation to engage in such play. These same events also elicit laughter in young human beings. For adults a good chase scene can add immensely to any action movie, especially if one of the cars in the chase is being driven by a chimp.

Some chimps are capable of conceptual play, in which they intentionally misuse visual or other tokens human beings have taught them. It is sort of a chimp joke. But if one chimp intentionally misuses the symbols in an attempt at joking, it simply confuses another chimp. The second chimp will not laugh, but will just look confused or become angry. Apparently chimps have no sense of humor, though they are good at playing. There are a few human beings like that.

Human response to laughter, Provine tells us, is typically involuntary and immediate. We can call it "contact laughter." We hear laughter and we laugh, just as when we hear or see yawning we begin to yawn. In some unusual cases laughter has led to "laugh jags," situations in which fairly large numbers of people have continued laughing semi-continuously for several weeks.

A well-studied laugh jag occurred in Tanzania in 1962. Individual bouts of laughter occasionally lasted for several hours, and were repeated periodically. The laugh epidemics started with schoolgirls, whose uncontrollable laughter led to the cancellation of classes. The children went home and soon the adult women in their homes were laughing uncontrollably also. These bouts were largely confined to groups of schoolgirls and some adult women. Historically this is not the only recorded case of such situations, but it is the most studied one. Could it be that there is something about male behavior that causes women and children to laugh? Nonsense.

Most people have had the experience of being in a group where laughter started, and once the group has stopped laughing, the slightest laugher-like sound will set the group off again. Once people are in a laughing mood, almost anything will set them off, including the memory of what set them off in the first place.[3]

This tendency to laugh when we hear others laugh has been ruthlessly exploited in the laugh track, a recent invention in which recorded laughter is played during a performance of some sort, usually advertised as comical or hilarious, to get the audience to start laughing and continue laughing. If the goal of the performance is only to produce laughter, it seems innocent enough, though it may obscure the fact that the performance is of questionable quality as far as humor is concerned. One can certainly see it might be a boon to a comedian or his writers who are painfully short of funny material. On the other hand the appearance of canned or artificial laughter not specifically related to the material may distort the judgment of the audience. However, if the audience is there simply to laugh, no matter how shallow the material, then it seems to be just one more misrepresentation in a society which daily bathes in the shallow surf of deception. And these days, most surf is polluted.[4]

The use of laugh tracks also suggests media leaders think that most people cannot tell what is funny, much less humorous, without being told. The apparent contempt the media people have for the state of awareness of the general public is clear. I suspect the readers of this book are exceptions to this dismal assumption.

Provine also examines laughter that seems to be caused by strictly physiological causes, and is therefore abnormal and unrelated to the environment, much less the apparent stimulus of the laughter. Alterations of the central nervous system, whether caused by an organic agent such as a virus, or by other physical damage, have been correlated with this kind of laughter. In addition, certain chemicals will produce laughter, the most notable of which is nitrous oxide, or "laughing gas." Strictly speaking, laughter may not be a gas, but it can be produced by a gas. Laughter in inappropriate situations tends to make some people uneasy. This is not a problem for some comedians, who often will use any technique to get laughter, including excessive profanity, bugger jokes, or references to passing gas. Sexual references have also historically been great crowd-pleasers.

The Distinction Between Laughter and Humor

The list of laughter in non-humorous situations is much larger than I have indicated, but the point to be established is that certain altered states of the brain can cause laughter that is inappropriate to the situation. This is clearly an area in which laughter can occur without humor, and occasionally without thought.

On the other hand, a person reading a humorous book alone in a room may enjoy the humor immensely, but not even smile. So we have humor without laughter. This is more understandable when we realize that laughter occurs mostly in social situations. People seldom laugh when they are alone.

So laughter can occur without humor, and humor can occur without laughter. This shows that there is no essential connection between the two.

To reinforce this belief that laughter and humor are certainly not necessarily connected, I will list some more normal occasions in which laughter occurs and humor may not be anywhere in the vicinity.

Occasions for Laughter

Laughter may occur in the simple presence of a delightful experience, and probably expresses exuberance and joy in living. That's a wonderful experience, but it isn't humor. Laughter may occur when there is a pleasant surprise, such as watching a magician or seeing an old friend. Watching a magician pull your old friend out of his hat may be really funny or laugh provoking. Laughter may occur during anticipation of an event that is likely to be fun. Laughter may result from a discovery of some sort, especially if the discovery is pleasant. But unhappy discoveries can induce laughter too, perhaps of a more nervous, even hysterical, nature. If the presence of a rattlesnake in a person's boot produces laughter, it is most likely hysterical laughter.

Laughter may occur from tickling, a traditional primate favorite, though this has limits for even the most dedicated practitioners. There is the laughter of relief, when one has been threatened and the event has not materialized or has been avoided. Some people laugh when they are embarrassed, nervous, or uncertain. Some people do this a good bit of the time, and we call this a "nervous laugh." Some people laugh at the discomfort of others, even the pain and death of others. Some people laugh when things that are difficult for them to acknowledge are brought up. Perhaps this is a variant on the nervous laugh.

Some people laugh at sex and religion. Some people laugh on the way to being executed. Some people have to suppress a tendency to laugh at funerals, with the possible exception of their own. Some people laugh at physiological abnormalities, either temporary or permanent, in other people. Some people laugh from mental derangement in the absence of detectable physiological abnormalities. Some people laugh because they feel superior to others. This list is but a sampling. There aren't many humorous or even comical things involved in the list.

With so many considerations, it is hard to believe that some highly intelligent and talented human beings have confused the behavior of laughter with the phenomenon of humor. However, I believe that is exactly what has happened, and that most early attempts to create a philosophy of humor were confused attempts to create a philosophy of laughter, and in a subsequent chapter I will give a brief history of the confusion.

Conclusion

Laughter is a type of behavior, and it is directly observable. Humor is a type of conscious realization, and therefore a primarily conceptual phenomenon. Observing humor is indirect. Experiencing it is not. Laughter and humor may be connected, but those connections are not simple. In other cases they may not be connected at all. Once we distinguish between laughter and humor, we are in a better position to understand the nature of a sense of humor.

One way to try to keep conceptually clear is to produce a set of stipulative definitions of the various key terms. These are sets of recommendations regarding how we ought to employ these terms for maximum clarity. It is probably true that few people will ever follow these recommendations, but the definitions are going to be made in the next chapter for the benefit of those people who want to think clearly with regard to these issues. Understanding can be its own reward, just like virtue.[5]

Endnotes

[1] I certainly never said it would be.

[2] Provine, Robert R. *Laughter: A Scientific Investigation.* New York, New York: Viking, 2000.

[3] Comedians love people who are in this frame of mind.

[4] It might be cheaper not to hire the comedian, and just pump nitrous oxide ("laughing gas") into the building.

[5] It has been said that virtue is its own reward, but sin pays better. I don't know who said it, but it wasn't I. Please note correct grammatical usage here. It's becoming rare.

Chapter 1: Laughter and Humor

"It's a small world, but I'd hate to paint it."

> *Stephen Wright*

"If absolute power corrupts, does absolute powerlessness make you pure?"

> *Harry Shearer*

Chapter 2

Definitions

If clear thinking is the goal, then control of the ordinary wildness of language is in order. While it might be common to present a brief glossary of terms, I will do more. Partly this is because I don't necessarily accept the definition of key terms as offered by the average dictionary. Dictionaries are often too imprecise for a number of reasons. They offer all the meanings a word might have, and which meaning is relevant in a given context may not be clear. Thus we have ambiguity.[1] Also, dictionaries do not necessarily try for a high degree of precision, often settling for synonyms that may be as unclear as the original word or words being defined. Moreover, the definitions may not be the most recent usages of a given word. Language is an organic entity that evolves. Dictionaries may lag in documenting this.

I am therefore going to stipulate the meanings I give to key terms, hoping thereby to gain some clarity and avoid confusion. While the meaning for a given term that I stipulate may be fairly close to a dictionary definition, it will be helpful if I explain in some cases why I am altering the definition a bit for my purposes. Hopefully, that will make my stipulated definition of the term more easily recognized and understood when it occurs.

Play

The first term to be considered is "play." Humor is simply a form of play, though there are many other forms of play. Play appears to be almost as important to people as sleep. We need to get away from the more serious aspects of life. We get tired. We need rest, and that often involves sleep. Sleep deprivation can be a form of torture. As a public service, this book is dedicated to the goal of putting the reader into a deep and satisfying sleep. What higher calling can an author have?[2]

People under stress or simply physically tired often seek play to give themselves or others a respite from the stress short of that which sleep can give. It is reported that people under the severe stress of being inmates in the Nazi concentration camps in World War II told each other jokes to relieve the tension, and even wrote and produced plays to distract themselves from the horror of their surroundings and possible fates.

So what is human play and where does it come from? Animals may play also, but considering that issue is beyond the scope of this inquiry. We have trouble enough as it is.

Let's start at the beginning. Infant human beings seem to be involved in random, and then exploratory behavior. Play in its earliest forms, as I am using the term, is spontaneous pleasurable behavior that can come under increasing conscious control, involving use of the body or mind to explore the physical or mental world. There is usually some sort of pleasure involved with these activities unless some other factor intervenes, and if there is some form of pleasure, the spontaneous activity is play. The child who has just put his finger in a light socket has had his play interrupted. Temporarily it is no longer pleasurable.

When I call play "spontaneous," I am accepting the theory of many psychologists that the propensity for some activities is built into our species (and other species too, of course). The proclivity for these activities used to be called instincts, but that word has fallen out of favor. My instincts tell me this is a loss, and not to use "instinct" in this sentence.

The brain, like the heart, seems to engage in periodic, ongoing activity. There seems to be no particular external stimulus for this activity. We can say it is a part of its nature.

The point is that infants begin very early to engage in some sort of activity, and that helps them learn what they can do and what their world is like. They can increasingly consciously control aspects of this behavior and therefore begin to control this world. They learn to use their bodies, and they soon begin to learn how to handle words and language. Once they master a set of concepts, which in itself is usually a pleasurable set of activities, they start exploring and playing with different combinations of these concepts.

For example, once a child has learned how to use the words "mama" and "bird" pretty comfortably, that child may come up with "Mama is a bird." This may cause considerable mirth in the child, and some pleasure in Mama in seeing the child happy and apparently learning, but the local Audubon Society is not going to be overly impressed. You have to start somewhere. This may be the kid's start of a career in comedy, humor, or ornithology. With any luck, it will be the latter. Or the career may be in philosophy, if the kid grows up to be an odd duck. But better an odd duck than a quack. I hope I can duck responsibility for that one. If I have to eat it, I may really be feeling "down in the mouth." So if that's offensive to you, bill me.

Play can be as simple as the enjoyment of the perception of sights, sounds, and other sensations. It consists in these cases of the delight in being able to perceive and identify what we are perceiving. Such perception may require minimal conceptual involvement. The successful and pleasurable uses of the senses can classify as play. In this case it may be simply the repetition of learned behavior for the pleasure involved in the process. Mastery of a skill can involve play. As we learn more about our world, our perceptions become more complex and sophisticated. We perceive more, and better.

Play is a pleasurable activity unless overdone. We all continue to play in various ways throughout our lives. We really can't help it. It seems to be useful, and is a behavior built into our DNA. Some of us just play better and more often than others.

Play can eventually be consciously controlled by the child. An attitude involved with seeking the pleasure of the behavior of play appears, indicating a habit has been formed. We can refer to this as a "playful attitude." Strong emotions, especially of a negative sort, will interfere with and sometimes make impossible the adoption of a playful attitude. A playful attitude in one form or another is carried into adulthood by most people, and is the foundation for a sense of humor. By that time in a human being's life, play has in most of its forms become very complex.

The ability to consciously choose to adopt this sense of play is important in the development of a sense of the funny, and ultimately of a sense of humor. I will say more about this shortly.

Amusement

Our next concept is that of amusement. Amusement is a

form of play. Amusement is the pleasant passing of time. In its simplest form, it can be the passive enjoyment of sights and sounds. In many cases little is being learned, but reinforcement of learning can be occurring.

We watch children at play, and we may be amused. Simple games can amuse. Various electronic devices can amuse us. Watching the lions eat Christians in the Colosseum could amuse, except for some people who may have been terribly concerned that the lions may be catching Mad Christian Disease.

Amusement comes in various wonderful and not so wonderful forms. It may not take much effort to be amused. The philosopher Thomas Hobbes[3] (1588-1679) noted that we can laugh and be amused at the difficulties and failures other people face because we feel superior to them. Amusement is often a relatively passive activity, though it can take a more active form of delight in, for example, the personal infliction of suffering upon another person. Human beings are not all that morally advanced, even today in our age of digital empathy.[4]

Entertainment

I am defining "entertainment" as intentional amusement. One person or group of people may put effort into amusing another person or group of people. The effort required to be entertained may be relatively small, so it is a relatively passive activity. If it takes a lot of effort to understand what is going on, it is most likely not very entertaining, or even amusing. People seeking amusement, or entertainment, usually don't want to put out a lot of effort. Amusement is recreation, not creation.

One exception to this may be in seeking aesthetic

experiences. It may take a great deal of concentration to fully appreciate a great work of art such as a symphony or play. Perhaps that is not recreation at all, but some other thing?

While it may be common to use amusement and entertainment as synonyms, I am not going to do so. One can be amused without being entertained, as in the example of watching children at play. The children have no intention of causing pleasure in anyone, but are simply wrapped up in their play. On the other hand, it follows from the definition of entertainment that if one is entertained, one is amused. Both entertainment and amusement are forms of play in that some at least minimal effort is being put forth to experience what is going on, and there is some sort of pleasure involved. In other words, the person being entertained or amused must be reasonably conscious and somewhat focused. Pleasure must be present in the mind of the person being amused or entertained or no amusement or entertainment is happening.

Laughter may occur at any of the levels of amusement or entertainment. People may laugh during play, during amusement, or during entertainment. There is another factor here, quite apart from amusement or entertainment. We tend to laugh when we hear others laugh. That's our old friend, contact laughter. Laughter is often cheap, and often at least somewhat beneficial, at least for the person doing the laughing.

Comedy

Now we come to comedy. Comedy is the attempt to provoke laughter in others. It is a form of entertainment, but not all forms of entertainment attempt to induce laughter, for example, magic. For a comedian laughter is usually his raison d'être, his excuse for living, his goal in life, his great hope, and that which will determine his status as a comedian. A non-comedic entertainer, on the other hand, may want to leave you pleasantly entertained, and he may do so with magic tricks, circus stunts, or any number of other activities in which we pass the time between the cradle and the grave. Amazement or astonishment may be the goal the non-comedic entertainer is seeking. Gasps may be more important than laughs.

We are about to pass into the realm of humor. Some comedians use humor in their quest for laughter. Suffice it to say that the line between the realms of comedy and of humor is not a hard and fast one, and it shifts from time to time. There are clear examples of humor and clear examples of comedy, and many examples in between where we can engage in amusing, even humorous, debates regarding whether a given example is humor or just comedy. Perhaps we will learn from each other during these debates.

As a side point, it is not unusual to have situations in which there are clear examples of two related categories, and intermediate cases between the two, as I maintain is the case between comedy and humor. A similar situation occurs between the visible colors. There are cases in which a color is clearly green, and other cases in which another color is clearly blue. There are numerous intermediate colors between green and blue, one blending into the other, and judging whether a given color is green or blue is difficult. The problem is not that we do not know what the terms "green" and "blue" denote, but whether the color in question should be called "green" or "blue." The woman in the family claims the color is green. The man calls it blue. The woman comments on the obvious insensitivity of the male of the species to nuances of color. People with a sense of humor don't need much more than this incongruity of judgment to grasp more of the incongruity of human life and the seemingly perpetual differences between men and woman, Mars and Venus, truth and error. The issue can take on cosmic significance.[5]

Humor

Humor as I understand it is the playful appreciation of incongruities, that is, the unexpected occurrences, surprises, ambiguities, inconsistencies, contradictions and paradoxes with which life confronts us all too often. Sometimes we notice these incongruities in the world, and sometimes we create incongruities. There is a difference, after all, between saying funny things, and saying things funny.

If we have a sense of humor, we don't just notice these incongruities; we appreciate them. A loose synonym for "appreciation" is "enjoyment," though some appreciation may not involve much enjoyment. The appreciation of the humorous usually occurs in an atmosphere of perceived safety. If an incongruity scares us to death, we are not likely to see the humor in the situation, at least not until the fear has subsided.

Finding a rattlesnake coiled up in our boot during a camping trip is an incongruity, but at the time the incongruity will not be appreciated. It may well be the source of laughter at a later time, when the story of the snake's location can take on a humorous dimension.

The concept of appreciation will be dealt with more fully in a later chapter, but briefly it is the process of recognizing the worth of something.

We must be in a playful state of mind to create or appreciate humor, and we can often choose to be in such a state. Once we are, there are many things one can do with an incongruity, and appreciating it is one.

Incongruity

Incongruities are all around us. A man slips on a banana peel. This is not what we expected, unless perhaps we planted the banana peel for that purpose. Then our laughter may be a bit sadistic. An evangelist who rails against adultery is caught in a motel room with his secretary, and their "Oh God" is not said prayerfully. Keep your eyes open. You just might experience an incongruity. Or you might experience yourself experiencing an incongruity. Stranger things have happened.

Since the concept of incongruity is crucial, it is a good time to provide as clear a definition of the term as I can. An incongruity is any occurrence, physical or mental, that does not fit in with our expectations at that time. The term "incongruity" is admittedly a vague term, and it is best left that way since I intend it to be a more general or generic term under which to fit or classify a rather diverse set of phenomena, and there may not be any one characteristic common to all of them.

By "incongruity" I mean the unexpected happenings, the ambiguities and inconsistencies of life, the absurdities, the paradoxes with which we are periodically surprised, annoyed, frightened, or delighted. Incongruity includes the ridiculous, the ludicrous, the irrational, and even the contradictory. Incongruities can upset plans and people, sometimes scare us, and in general may require adjustments in our thinking or behavior. If you are a person inclined to underline important passages in a book, you might consider underlining the stipulative definition of incongruity just given. Or at least make a mark in the margin.[6]

One way to deal with incongruities is to treat them humorously. What that means is that a person appreciates or enjoys the incongruity in a playful state of mind, and has in many cases made a habit of doing so.

Defining a sense of humor is not easy. That is a major goal of this book. It will take a while to have the conceptual apparatus in place to understand it. Defining other terms and rejecting theories is just a step toward that goal. You were probably waiting for me to make that confession.

Humor is marked in part by the effort involved in the exploration and appreciation or enjoyment of incongruity. The laughter hopefully evoked by comedy seems to be essential to comedy, even if it may be laughter inspired by the laughter of others only, or "contact laughter." Humor may not provoke laughter at all. We may smile, wince, grin or chuckle to ourselves quietly. We may be reading a humorous book, and never crack a smile. What is certain is that we will be putting some effort into understanding the humor and appreciating the incongruity that is being explored.

Humor involves our intellectual or conceptual capacities. Comedy often merely requires a level of consciousness that may be entirely passive or non-active. Listening to two people calling each other names in a sitcom does not require much intellectual capacity unless the two people are expert at it, or the writers have produced an extremely good dialogue. In that case a connoisseur of insults may be keenly appreciative.

Plus, comedy may not involve the exploration of incongruity at all. This is often the case with contact laughter provoked by the laughter of others. Another example is that of a comedian known for saying a certain phrase, such as "he has no life." He may get laughs just with the phrase itself. People expect the phrase to be used, and he is likely not to disappoint. We laugh partly or even wholly due to the comfort of fulfilled expectations. But that is a laugh nevertheless, and that is what the comedian wants.

It is well to keep in mind that comedians can also use humor to provoke laughter, and the good ones do that fairly often.

Humor is harder to appreciate than comedy, and some people don't bother to appreciate the humor in a situation. They may be the truly humorless, but in their own way they can be quite humorous. The paradox of a thinking, feeling being who is not going to think and feel very deeply has possibilities for humor, and for tragedy.

Of course there may be reasons why a person is not up to tackling a specific bout of either comedy or humor. Fatigue, perhaps, or lack of time. Maybe the subject matter is hitting too close to home, is upsetting, and objectivity is lacking. Or it may be that the person has never been taught to appreciate humor, since a sense of humor is a learned phenomenon and some people seem to have not learned it.

Surprise and the Persistence of Humor

It has been claimed by some that surprise is the essence of comedy and humor and not just a commonly occurring characteristic. While surprise may be caused by many examples of comedy and humor, it is not essential. Some incongruities are surprising and some are not. It depends in part on the individual who perceives the incongruity. What surprises one person may bore another.

If surprise were an essential element in humor, we would be hard pressed to explain the phenomenon of repeated enjoyment of the same example of humor. It is hard to be surprised a second and a third time a person experiences a particular example of the amusing. The person knows what is coming once he has experienced it, and surprise, if present at all, is minimal. The level of delight, or at least of appreciation, can remain quite high, or even increase. We will call this phenomenon "The Persistence of Humor."

It is also a fact based on the experience of many people that the same work of art can be experienced many times and still be enjoyed, in many cases enjoyed more in later encounters than in the first or second one. This adds a line of argumentation to the assertion, to be argued for more thoroughly in Chapter 4, that humor is a type of aesthetic experience, since many examples of humor will allow for many repetitions without losing their humorous quality. Subsequent exposure to the humorous material may even increase the appreciation involved.

We might even use as a criterion for the excellence of an example of humor the fact that a given possible example of humor continues to delight or move the majority of people who spend time enjoying and understanding it.

We often make a similar claim about something we judge to be an excellent work of art in the traditional sense, but I certainly don't want to tip my hand at this point.

The Funny

No doubt some of you are saying to yourself, "This is not very funny. Not very funny at all. It's difficult." Perhaps. It depends on what you mean by "funny." I propose that we use the adjective "funny" to denote anything that is capable of causing laughter. "Fun" denotes the experience of encountering the funny in a playful way. By these definitions almost anything you can name can be funny, and can be the object of fun. It may depend on your sense of humor. But you most likely expected that.

So potentially the universe and everything in it are funny. With such a supply of potentially laughable objects, it's hard to take the universe very seriously, or at least to take it seriously most of the time. One humorist made the observation that there is no evidence that the world or life in it is the least bit serious. That leaves the door open for the universe to be funny, though it might be neutral and depend on us to perceive it as serious or funny. Which perspective do you prefer?

The latter is a humble example of a philosophical question. I thought I ought to point that out so that you don't miss it. It has absolutely no significance with regard to anything I am doing here.

Funny-ha-ha and Funny-peculiar

Actually the situation is not that simple. There are two sorts of "funny": Funny-ha-ha and funny-peculiar. Funny-ha-ha denotes anything that tends to excite positive laughter, that is, laughter associated with pleasure. Funny-peculiar denotes a situation in which the laughter is not associated with pleasure, such as situations that tend to excite nervous, confused, or hysterical laughter. A person laughing during the exploration of a haunted house at an amusement park may be laughing as the consequence of nervousness and confusion, and not as a consequence of pleasure.

Laughing on the way to the gallows may not involve much amusement, at least for the guest of honor. But it should be noted that being hung up can cure you of all your hang-ups.[7]

I am using the term "pleasure" broadly, to denote not only powerful feelings such as the overwhelming experience of orgasm, which I believe is just about the strongest momentary pleasure of which a human being is capable, to the faintest tingle of a positive sort, such as the smell of a rose, or the touch of a butterfly gently landing on your finger, looking pensively at you and wondering, in its own butterfly way, why you are about to crush it.

Such is the life of a butterfly. And of a philosopher of humor.

Incongruity can be as simple as taking a thought train onto a new track, one that most people did not anticipate and find (get this) incongruous. It can be simple exaggeration, especially if well done. Incongruity is the essence of humor, but there is nothing humorous about incongruity in and of itself. It takes a sense of humor to transform a simple incongruity into the stuff of humor, and to appreciate that transformation. That is why understanding a sense of humor is our ultimate goal.

Conclusion

I've stipulated the definitions of a number of key terms, and tried to clarify some conceptual issues. You now have enough theory and hopefully clarity of definition to be hopelessly befuddled by the following chapters. I know I am.

Endnotes

[1] Ambiguity also sets up the possibility for a pun, for which it is justifiably celebrated in song and story.

[2] Some day you'll thank me. Maybe when you wake up?

[3] Hobbes, Thomas. *Leviathan*. Part I, Chapter 6, and in *Human Nature* Chapter 8. We haven't heard the last of Thomas Hobbes, though he has.

[4] Digital empathy? Sure. We have digital everything else, so why not empathy? It's easier than normal empathy.

[5] The color in question is blue, however. No doubt about it.

[6] When you rediscover that mark, you'll probably be puzzled about why it is there in the first place.

[7] I, however, have way too much class to make such a claim.

"I didn't attend the funeral, but I sent a nice letter saying I approved of it."

Mark Twain

"Never have children, only grandchildren."

Gore Vidal

Chapter 3
Theoretical Underpinnings

Under the topic of theoretical underpinnings, I am making good on my earlier promise to provide a brief historical background. After this I advance one important thesis of this book, which is that a sense of humor is one form of a sense of the aesthetic. If you prefer a weaker claim, I indicate that a sense of humor can be most easily understood by comparing it with a sense of the aesthetic

It is not my intention to get into theoretical battles with proponents of some of the classical or contemporary views regarding the nature of the causes of laughter. Nevertheless, an attempt to point out what I consider to be errors in their thinking may clarify the positions I'm developing. This involves more complex theoretical analysis. Those who can stand it should just hold their collective noses and plow ahead. Actually, holding any nose will do. It doesn't have to be your own. That is an ancient mistake, and the sooner we get rid of it, the better we will all be for it. The nose will have to be liberated, sooner or later, and I hope to be running on the cutting edge of that revolution. That is a difficult undertaking, as anyone who has been doing such running knows.[1]

I'm not examining every position that has ever been held, but some are particularly interesting. There are adequate histories of the theories and their problems in other books. I simply intend to point out the inadequacy of some theories, especially if they have been influential or have a part of the truth. This means I will drop a few names along the way. Dropping names doesn't hurt. They rarely break.

Some will say that this section belongs earlier in the

book. Some will say it should be later. I didn't want it to set too heavy a tone early in the book, so I put it here, where it is easy to skip over.

Again, let me stress the significance of a clear distinction between humor (a mental phenomenon) and laughter (a physical behavior, behind which there may in some cases be almost no mental processes). One major point in this chapter is that most of the major historical theories are not theories of humor at all, but are theories regarding the causes of laughter. I am not the first to make this claim, and I most likely will not be the last. If I am correct in this assertion, many of the classical theories are conceptually confused, and present only a part of the picture. The proponents of a theory often think they are talking about humor when they are actually dealing with laughter and some of its causes.

There are three classical theories of laughter in those extremely small circles where people are concerned with these issues. I am taking them up in no particular order.

Superiority Theory

An old timer is the Superiority Theory, often associated with the name of Thomas Hobbes (1588-1679), previously mentioned. Having been dead for some centuries, he is not likely to be offended by criticism of his position. He claimed that we laugh because we feel superior to other people, institutions, or ideas. This is a bit of an oversimplification of the theory, but it is all we need to show its inadequacies, though it seems correct in a small number of cases. We do sometimes laugh because we feel superior to someone or something.

Please note that the Superiority Theory is about what

we sometimes laugh at, not about what is humorous. Hobbes claimed that we laugh because we feel superior to others and often to their lower status compared with our own. The laughter of ridicule is a good example of this sort of laughter. Laughter expresses our feelings of superiority. Incidentally, some comedians cultivate this type of laughter in their audience, and we can sometimes classify comedians by the kind of laughter they seek in their jokes.

To show the inadequacy of Hobbes' theory, we need to realize that we laugh at many other things too, for example, at situations that delight us, and many of them are not humorous. Also we don't laugh at some occasions that are humorous. In addition, we may not laugh when we feel superior to another person, group of persons, or their ideas or institutions, for any number of reasons, one of which may be fear. The people or their beliefs that we might be inclined to laugh at may be powerful, and might do us harm. We may be afraid to laugh, or be constrained by ethical considerations, in situations in which we feel quite superior to another person, group, or their ideas. Cruelty is not particularly pretty, though it can be fun. There are numerous examples of officially sanctioned cruelty throughout human history, and plenty of participants in the activity.

So we laugh for many reasons that have nothing to do with feeling superior. The nervous laugh of a frightened person has nothing to do with feelings of superiority. Some philosophers have a tendency to make one example into a theory about the whole of the phenomena they are explaining. Hobbes, I believe, did this. This produces a theory that is incomplete, and in Hobbes' case, a theory that is also confused. If some people confuse this theory of what we laugh at with a theory of humor, their theory is inadequate as well as incomplete.

I claim no originality in this analysis of Hobbes' theory. Other philosophers have pointed these problems out, and they have also done so with regard to the other theories I am about to discuss.[2]

Incongruity Theory

A second of the classical theories claims we laugh at things that involve incongruity. We can associate the German philosophers Immanuel Kant (1724-1804) and Arthur Schopenhauer (1788-1860) historically with this theory, although others made attempts to elaborate or modify it. The two philosophers cited held similar but not identical views. I will not cover all forms of Incongruity Theory. To understand the nature of this theory, we can consider this oversimplified presentation. It involves our intellectual or emotional pleasure at the discovery of an incongruity in the world and our successful understanding or resolution of that incongruity.

A pig dropping from the sky is certainly something quite unexpected and incongruous. To discover that this particular pig has a talent for climbing trees, but in this instance has slipped and fallen, immediately resolves the confusion caused by the incongruity. This porcine incongruity is not particularly laughable in and of itself, but it could be the subject of humorous incongruity in the right circumstances. The late British philosopher, Montgomery Python,[3] worked fairly successfully with the idea.

I think there is merit in the positions of Kant and Schopenhauer, which do seem to be theories about the nature of humor as well as theories about what we laugh at. Suffice it to say that "incongruity" needs to be carefully defined, as I did in a previous chapter, and much more needs to be said about the attitude of the person appreciating or creating humor. Incongruities that are frightening tend to excite no laughter, or at best nervous laughter, and thus tell us very little about humor. Humor seems to require some sort of positive orientation toward the world at the point at which the incongruity is encountered or created. You have to be in a playful mood to create or appreciate humor. You can have the bejesus scared out of you any old time.

Some form of Incongruity Theory seems to me to cover the requirements of a good theory of humor, and I will develop what seems to me to be the most comprehensive form of the theory later.

Relief Theory

The third classical theory of the nature of humor is often identified with Sigmund Freud (1856-1939). It is called Relief Theory since it claims that people laugh when they feel pleasure, or at least relief, as some sort of psychological restraint is removed from them, and they can dissipate, in the form of laughter, the energy they were using to deal with or repress the restraint.

No doubt people do laugh in such circumstances, and the application of a massively complex Freudian psychoanalytic apparatus can make the theory truly fearsome. At best, this is a form of laughter theory having little to do with humor. It provides us with another theory about why we laugh. We laugh because nervous energy is no longer needed to repress or deal with something, and is released and expresses itself in the behavior of laughter. We laugh as a consequence of being exposed to whatever it is that allows the release. Certain kinds of material seem to do this pretty well. Consider slapstick jokes and sexual humor. Consider combining the two. Consider sado-masochism for fun and profit.

It won't hurt to mention the previously observed philosophical tendency to take one case and make it central to the development of a theory. Relief Theory helps to explain why off-color jokes or simple profanity often get laughs. Profanity, however, is seldom humorous, though it can be. People laugh at profanity for a number of reasons, the main one of which is nervousness. Another reason people laugh at profanity and sexual jokes is relief from the restraints society imposes with regard to certain words and other behavior. Damn it, the theory has some value.

The comedian who makes a living with profanity as his main trick is usually a pretty shallow comedian. He may get laughs, and that may be all he wants. Nervous laughter is indeed one form of laughter, and perhaps one form is as good as any in some people's opinions.

Relief Theory claims that we are uncomfortable with the restraints placed on us by society, not only with regard to sex, and profanity, but also violence. We expend a lot of energy restraining our violent tendencies as well as our sexual interests. Laughter gives us at least symbolic relief from the pressure caused by the restraints. We express in laughter the energy we do not temporarily need to utilize to control ourselves. Hence we are attracted to sexual humor and to humor involving aggression. Slapstick humor has always had its advocates, and this theory explains why. Shades of *The Three Stooges*!

Sadomasochistic humor ought to be a real barnburner.

Could it be that sadomasochists like to burn barns? Especially if someone they don't like is in the barns?

There is also repression of expression involved with topics other than sex and violence. Some words are banished, or at least the attempt is made. The so-called "N-word" involves neither explicit sex nor explicit violence, yet there have been attempts to exterminate it from our vocabulary for decades. For many people its use is degrading. Why the word "Nihilist" would be considered so upsetting escapes me, but if you hear the word said out loud, there will most likely be a bout of nervous laughter immediately following it. Relief Theory in its various forms tries to account for that laughter.[4]

I'm not even going to mention the "F-bomb." Being a Federalist used to be a perfectly acceptable political position. Of course combining the F-word with other words is also taboo. Why being a person who makes maternity clothes is so bad, I just don't understand. Being a mother-frocker is an important job.

I suspect you may have found the explanation of the "N-word" as "Nihilist" presented you with an incongruity. You expected something else. Incongruity strikes again. We are up to our collective clavicles in incongruities all the time. We just don't notice most of them. Those with a mind-set to notice incongruities and to play with the possibilities for humor can see them as humorous. That is partly what a sense of humor involves, you mother-frocker.

For decades, various sitcoms have fed the public a steady diet of sometimes comical and usually cruel put-downs of one spouse by another, or of one sex by the other. This is clearly verbal aggression. Hobbes would have loved it.

I can only speculate about why people laugh at this, but it seems to indicate a low level of psychological intimacy in many marriages and friendships. Perhaps the actors in the sitcoms portray what the viewing audience only wishes they could say to each other, and the repressed persons get some relief from that.

I suppose that verbal abuse of a spouse or a friend is preferable to physical abuse. Perhaps the symbolic abuse portrayed on the TV screen helps keep the abuse level from escalating physically in the relationships of the viewers? After all, many people have hundreds, even thousands of friends on Facebook, and sacrificing a few may be justifiable by the sheer overabundance of friends? You be the judge on this one. I have no way of proving the theory either way.

The various forms of Relief Theory lack sufficient generality. They do not cover all the situations in which we laugh or in which we find humor. They do apply to some.

The Humorous and the Aesthetic

More recent theories regarding the nature of humor, developed by several philosophers, hold that there is a connection between the aesthetic and the humorous.[5] In its strongest form, the theory holds that the experience of the humorous is simply one type of the experience of the aesthetic. Though I accept this theory, there are a number of problems associated with it. I will deal with only one at this point.

One problem in developing this position, or at least one form of it, is the belief that there is a specific aesthetic emotion, and likewise a specific humorous emotion. I cannot locate a specific, unique aesthetic emotion, or a specific, unique humorous emotion, sometimes called "mirth" by those who develop the theory. It seems to me this is a question of introspection, and I can introspect no such emotion, or even a set of related emotions. Many other people report a similar failure to introspect that aesthetic or that humorous emotion.

For example, in the last scene in Hamlet, the stage is filled with dying people and former people, not the least of which is Hamlet. Is there another emotion beyond the sorrow, the sense of fate, the sense that human life is indeed a fragile thing, and death so close to all of us? If so, I missed it. There were plenty of emotions already.

This theory states that there is one and the same special aesthetic emotion experienced when one views the tragic play "Death of a Salesman," or listens to Beethoven's majestic symphonies, or contemplates a Mondrian canvas with its geometrical precision, or follows the machinations of Mozart's opera *The Magic Flute*. If there is such a single emotion, I've never found it, and many other people make the same claim. Perhaps it is too well hidden among the other emotions that might be felt in the experience of a work of art? Or perhaps it is not there at all?

I believe there is no such single aesthetic emotion. I'm not going to fake an emotion for the sake of a theory.

Could it be that this aesthetic emotion is really just a specific emotion, such as sorrow, experienced in an aesthetic context? The stage is not real life, but is there some sort of aesthetic sorrow distinct from "real" sorrow, the sorrow we feel for real people when they die, for example? Or is it simply that some sorrow affects us very personally and deeply, and some is less personal, as when we hear of the death of a distant friend, or a relative we never much cared for, or a person whose life has inspired us, but whom we never knew personally? It appears to me that there are just degrees of sorrow, not different kinds of sorrow. I don't think there is a uniquely aesthetic sorrow, but just degrees of intensity of the emotion that is dependent on the context.

There is no sorrow at all that I can find in Beethoven's Ninth Symphony. So the special aesthetic emotion does not seem to be a specific type of emotion, but some sort of general aesthetic emotion in addition to the rest. I still cannot find it.

Likewise I find no common humorous emotion when appreciating the comedy of Molière, the essays of P.G. Wodehouse, the musical antics of Victor Borge, or the cinematic perils of Buster Keaton. In all these cases there is often a feeling of delight, but not always. There may be laughter, but not always. Perhaps that so-called humorous emotion is, in reality, delight and not some specifically humorous emotion? However, a humorous verbal attack on a person may have no delight involved with it for us, especially, for instance, if the person being attacked is a good friend of ours. Or if the attack is directed toward our personal epidermis.

It is also hard to use the word "delight" to describe the feelings generated by a great tragedy such as Macbeth.

I conclude there is no such unique humorous emotion in all these examples of comedy or humor. What I do detect is not a commonality of emotion, but a set of attitudes that make the appreciation of art, and of humor, possible. Emotions are short-lived, largely physiological phenomena, lingering in consciousness for a short time. Attitudes are long-term psychological structures that direct perception and our understanding and expectations with regard to what we perceive. This is the way in which I am going to use the two concepts of emotion and attitude. By these standards, it would be hard to imagine what an aesthetic or a humorous emotion might be.

So while I cannot agree that there is either a distinctly aesthetic emotion, or a distinctly humorous emotion, I think this theory offers some ideas worth pursuing. No doubt, aesthetic appreciation and humor appreciation involve emotions, sometimes very intense emotions, but the goal of both is not simply the excitation of emotion. You can excite emotions in yourself by simply picking your nose. You can cause strong emotions in others by simply picking your nose in public. Or someone else's nose in public. The aesthetic and the humorous have much more they can accomplish in the symphony of human life than the excitation of an emotion or group of emotions. The simple excitation of emotions, especially familiar ones, is the province of entertainment, not of the aesthetic or the humorous.

The example of nose picking above, attentive readers know, is the presentation of yet another example of incongruity. No one expected a discussion of nose picking in the middle of a somewhat complex philosophical discussion. But incongruity comes in many colors, including the use of surprising, even disgusting examples to make a point. The point is that there is more to aesthetics, and also to humor, than eliciting strong emotions, whether there is a unique aesthetic emotion, or humorous emotion, or not.

Those with a slightly akimbo sense of humor may have

already pushed my example further. Some may have envisioned Olympic competition in nose picking. Some have wondered whether it would be an individual or a team sport. Some may have started to pursue the argument that if synchronized swimming is an Olympic sport, why not synchronized nose picking? Those whose minds are polluted with a sense of humor of this sort are to be congratulated. You are indeed the pick of the litter.

Puns qualify as humor on Tuesdays and Thursdays, but not on other days. Check your calendar for further details. Please also note that leap years may give you an extra day for punning. Use it wisely.

Conclusion

We've explored some philosophical considerations involving several of the older theories in this chapter, and found them to be incomplete in one way or another. We also considered the theory that there is a unique aesthetic emotion, and analogically one temporary emotion that is associated with some forms of laughter. None of these theories is adequate to explain much about humor. Now we need to clear up some other misunderstanding before we focus on the aesthetic.

Endnotes

[1] I am not the least bit sorry for that one. You got yourself into this.

[2] There is an extensive discussion of the history of various attempts to produce both a theory of laughter and a theory of humor, though that distinction is not important to most of the people discussing this history. A good recent discussion of this history can be found in Morreal, John. *Comic Relief: A Comprehensive Philosophy of Humor*, Chichester, West Sussex, UK: Wiley-Blackwell, 2009.

[3] There is no such philosopher as Montgomery Python. I'm kidding, as is sometimes my wont. There was a British comedy team known as "Monty Python," and the pig sketch is theirs.

[4] Were you expecting some other N-word?

[5] Among those pursuing this line of thinking is D. H. Monro in "Humor" in the *Encyclopedia of Philosophy,* Volume 4, p.90. First Edition edited by Paul Edwards. New York: Macmillan, 1967. John Morreall also considers it in "Humor and Aesthetic Experience," *Journal of Aesthetic Education,* Vol. 15, January 1981, pp 55-70. University of Illinois Press. Now if that isn't a set of obscure academic references, I don't know what is. This is about as esoteric as I'm going to get.

"Life is far too important a thing ever to talk seriously about."

Oscar Wilde

"Men and women belong in different species, and communication between them is still in its infancy."

Bill Cosby

"Beauty is in the eye of the beer holder."

Richard "Kinky" Friedman

Chapter 4
Humor, Beauty, and Taste

There are more philosophical issues to clarify. There is some confused thinking prevalent in conversations and writings involving the aesthetic and the humorous. Clarifying some of this confusion is the goal of this chapter.

For the sake of clarity, we need some labels. The issues to be discussed are labeled "The Relativity of Beauty, Humor, and Taste," "Developed Taste," and "Liking and Knowing Something is Good." The labels will help keep the issues straight.

I am keeping the questions involving beauty and the aesthetic in general, and the issues of humor, connected in these discussions. This is because I think humor is a subset of the category of the aesthetic, as is beauty. (There are aesthetic events or objects that are not beautiful, but most of the discussions are focused on beauty.) Even if someone does not accept my classification of the humorous as a class within the aesthetic, the similarities between these areas can help make my position clearer.

The Relativity of Beauty, Humor, and Taste

This is a delightful conceptual snarl, "delightful" to a philosopher who likes to unravel conceptual snarls. It occurs occasionally when beauty or humor is discussed. More insidiously, relativity of taste is a common assumption that is rarely examined, so its inadequacies are rarely displayed. It is the claim that both beauty and humor are "relative." It is often used to shut down discussions about the value of a work of art, or of a piece of humor, when there is disagreement about quality or comparative worth. The disputants are reminded that "it's relative," or better yet, "it's all relative." These claims are delivered with an air of triumph at having clarified the issue, resolved the silliness of the dispute, and established the intellectual and moral superiority of the person pointing out the relativity.

Sometimes the word "subjective" is substituted for the word "relative," and a really skilled arguer can use both words in the discussion, and sometimes in the same sentence. Such are the joys of being conceptually ambidextrous. If you have never seen this type of bogus resolution of a potentially good discussion, all I can say is "you should have been there."

The claim that judgments in the arts or humor are relative or subjective rests on the observation that people do disagree on questions of beauty and humor. If that is all that this claims means, there is really no issue. People do indeed disagree. That's a fact. What does it prove? That's the question.

Even if there is disagreement, nothing is established except the fact of disagreement. It is certainly true that people differ in their aesthetic judgments and judgments regarding the humorous. In addition, the same person may not perceive something as beautiful or humorous today that he thought was beautiful or humorous yesterday. In that respect he can be said to disagree with himself. If this is all that relativity of judgment means, it is acknowledged that judgments are "relative."[1]

In addition it may be implied or asserted that agreement in such disputes is impossible, there are no real standards beyond personal experience, and the attempt to establish agreement is pointless. This is a more serious claim. The implication is that once people disagree on these sorts of issues, there is nothing more of any significance to be said.

There may be additional muttering about how "tastes" are simply that, and so true judgments of worth or value cannot be made when there is disagreement. Or even if there is no disagreement. The principle of non-resolution of "subjective" judgments, or judgments involving "taste," may be stated in Latin, making it even more imposing to anyone but a Roman. Or a Catholic priest.

"De gustibus non disputandum est." Even Julius Caesar knew that.[2]

Calling the judgments "relative" or "subjective," as opposed to "absolute" or "objective," is supposed to finish the issue, since "subjective" is the word applied to judgments for which there are no well-established procedures for resolution. Judgments regarding beauty and humor are included in this category. This is usually contrasted with "objective" issues, paradigmatically issues in science.[3] If a person claims that water is a compound of hydrogen and nitrogen, there are scientific procedures that resolve the question absolutely, objectively, and for good. On the other hand, if someone claims that the taste of the water from a particular source such as "Oldbed Springs" is superior, the best we can do is roll our eyes. Or so it is claimed. We might do a taste test, but according to the claim, that would just lead to more disagreement.

The use of the word "taste" here is confusing. There is one sense of "taste," which we can call "physical taste." This is taste that denotes a sensation in the mouth, involving of course our friend the brain. To say, "that's salty," or more accurately, "That tastes salty to me," truthfully reported, can only be disputed by a mad man or someone just looking for an argument. You cannot dispute how something strikes the palate of an honest reporter. He could lie, of course, but why bother? Taste in this sense is a physiological and psychological reaction.

It is claimed that some people like dry martinis, some do not, and it is just a matter of "taste," which is notoriously subjective. You cannot really argue whether a very dry martini is better than one not so dry, or even that the taste of any martini is good. Likewise some people like green olives and some do not. We can expand the list to a very long one, risking terminal boredom on the part of the reader. Or the writer.

I agree completely with the observations involving physical taste. It's all in a person's tongue, and of course in his head, where the tongue often resides. It is interesting that the brain resides there too.

The other sense of taste, involved with, among other areas, the aesthetic or the humorous, is also "subjective," meaning it involves a judgment about some issue that cannot be resolved objectively or scientifically. People do, from time to time, try to resolve these issues somewhat objectively on the basis of a majority vote. "The *Mona Lisa* is great. Ten million Frenchmen can't be wrong." This is simply an appeal to popular beliefs, since ten million people of any group can be completely wrong, and have been on occasion. The judgment of ten million people believing the earth is flat does not in the least affect the shape of the earth.

This second sense of "taste" we can call "evaluative taste," although that label is somewhat misleading. It is the best I can do. I do not wish to imply that judgments of "evaluative" taste cannot be intelligently discussed.

I want to contrast evaluative taste with physical taste, which requires no evaluation and is simply a report of an experience of one or more of the senses.

A Beethoven piano concerto can be reported as "loud." That is a simple sensory report. That is the way it was heard by one person, and maybe more. It can also be reported as "majestic," or "pompous." Now we are dealing with evaluative taste, and perhaps some industrial-strength disagreements.

The mistaken debate concerning taste claims that it is useless to argue about the characteristics or the value of one work of art, or example of humor, because it involves the exercise of "taste." Most people are supposed to know that judgments of taste cannot be refuted or even sensibly discussed. If you think something is salty, then that's the end of the discussion. If you like "The Lumberjack Song" of Monty Python, fine. But it is not better or worse than "The Philosophers' Song."

What we have here is what philosophers call an equivocation. It is the act of changing from one meaning of a term, in this case "taste," to a different but perhaps related use of the term in the same argument. In this case it is switching from the first meaning to the term "taste" as a physical sensation, to the other meaning of "taste" as an issue of judgment sometimes involving complex questions. Physical taste is one thing. Judgment about potentially resolvable issues is quite another. To use the word "taste" in referring to both kinds of taste, without noting the difference in meaning, simply confuses the issue. Confusion is the goal of any equivocation. It is also the last refuge of a scoundrel.

There are ways to deal with disputes involving this second

sense of the word "taste," and I will get to them. There are, to repeat for the purpose of contrast, no reasonable disputes involved when the first sense of taste, physical taste, is involved. There are reasonable and perhaps resolvable debates when the second sense of taste is involved.

Thus, attempts to throttle aesthetic and humorous debate by reference to "taste" depend on a logical mistake and can be dismissed once they are understood.

Similar considerations are involved in the use of the term "relative," though no obvious equivocation is involved. Claiming judgments of value are relative is simply the factual observation that people often disagree about questions of value, as was previously observed. This is simply a claim involving factual observations with no obvious implications, including that such judgments cannot be intelligently discussed and perhaps resolved.

I think we can agree that people do make different judgments about beauty, and of course, humor. That's an observable fact. However, in most if not all cases, an informed judgment is better than an uninformed judgment. The point is that disagreement does not prove the disagreement is irresolvable, and therefore debate is senseless. Differing judgments on an issue like beauty, or the humorous quality of something, do not in the least establish that none of the judgments are right or wrong, or at least better or more poorly supported.

The word "subjective," or better yet, "radically subjective," is used in the same way to undermine intelligent discussion of experiences and judgments. It rests on the assumption that the only states that exist are either the reality of physical taste or the exact judgments of the sciences. There is, of course, a tremendous range of middle ground assertions, and this is where judgments involving both humor and beauty are located.

Developed Taste

In cases of beauty and humor we can introduce the notion that some people have "good taste" and others have "bad taste," or as I prefer to say, "developed taste" and "undeveloped taste." People with developed taste can make "informed judgments" on these issues. Another way to put it would be to talk of "educated taste" and "uneducated taste," though there are certainly degrees of both, and it is not an all or nothing issue. If this has an elitist ring to it, that is unfortunate, but it needn't have that ring. We are simply saying that some people's judgment, formed by study and experience, is better than the judgment of people with little study and experience in that field.

The claim that the judgment of people with good taste is better than the judgment of people with poor or no taste can clarify this problem of differing judgments. There is a cliché that says good taste is timeless. The problem is in identifying which judgments involve good taste, and this is partly a question of the experience and sensitivity of the judge. It is equally true that bad taste is timeless. But in many areas, and not just aesthetics, education and experience enhance judgment.

The judgment of someone who has studied at a good medical school to be a brain surgeon and has considerable experience in the field is better than someone who has read "Brain Surgery for Dummies." Which one would you want fiddling around in your cranium? I don't really care which one works cheaper.

Back to humor. It is certainly true that people make different judgments about what is humorous, or how humorous something is compared with other examples of humor. I am claiming that good or informed judgment is better than bad or uninformed judgment in deciding these issues. We need to explore this issue of the nature of judgment involving good taste, whether in art or in humor.

Liking and Knowing Something is Good

A related issue that will bring more clarity is a discussion of the distinction between liking something and knowing something is good. Someone may really, really like Playboy centerfolds, but if he is unacquainted with Michelangelo's ceiling of the Sistine Chapel, or any other work of similar quality, his judgment of what he likes is impeccable, but his judgment about what is good is not worth much. That latter judgment is peccable.[4]

It takes little effort to like something. It takes little effort to discover what one likes. Self-congratulation for this achievement is best held to a minimum. No end zone dances, please, though you might want to high-five yourself. What is the sound of one hand high-fiving? That's an old philosophical puzzle.

There is a distinction between liking something and knowing it is good. Therefore it is possible for someone to like something, but know it is not good. Or to not like something he knows is good. A person may not like operas, but may have enough experience to tell a good one from a mediocre one, for instance. It's a bit unusual for people to develop expertise in an area in which they have little interest. Sufficient money can modify this, however.

Accepting the judgment of those people who can judge what is good independently of what they like or dislike can often go far in resolving disputes. This is true with regard to both beauty and humor. Let's leave the issue of what "good" means in these contexts unexamined. We have enough troubles as it is.

We still have the issue of comparing one aesthetic object, or one example of humor, with another. Is the *Mona Lisa* a better painting than Salvador Dali's painting, *The Persistence of Memory*?

Let's bring in John Stuart Mill's (1806-1873) contention, rephrased here, that in order to know if one aesthetic object is better than another, you need the judgment of someone who appreciates both. In comparing Beethoven's *Ninth Symphony* with "My Melancholy Baby," a person should be able to appreciate both Beethoven and "My Melancholy Baby." It would certainly be worth the effort to develop one's taste so one can appreciate Beethoven's *Ninth Symphony*, if the experience caused by Beethoven's creation is superior in some ways to that caused by "My Melancholy Baby."

The past experience of a drunk in a bar, listening with what is left of his senses to "My Melancholy Baby," and perhaps remembering a few melancholic babies, is not good enough to support a comparative judgment. For him, an enjoyment of "My Melancholy Baby" is the only foundation for his judgment. To know which is the better experience, you have to know and appreciate both. Comparisons are pointless if the person doing the comparison does not know all the objects being compared. There is a difference between a fifth and the *Ninth*. But you have to know a bit about an augmented seventh to appreciate that difference.[5]

To advance our comparison between beauty and humor, we assume that humor, like beauty, is not a feature of our world. Incongruity, which is the foundation of humor, depends in part on the mind. It is related to the assumptions and attitudes of the individual. This is to say that what is incongruous to one person may not be incongruous to another. What is incongruous to one person at one time may not be incongruous to that person at another time.

Even if two people have assumptions and attitudes that are very similar, it does not follow they will detect or create the same incongruities. Some people are more observant than others, more tuned in to the incongruities of our world. This is partly a cultivated ability, and some people choose to cultivate it more completely than do other people. Some people are more creative and therefore more likely to create humor, or to create more humor.

Also two very similar people will have differing experiences from which to draw the incongruities. That will influence the issue of what incongruities they notice or create.

Thus appreciating or judging the quality of an incongruity will depend directly on whether an individual experiences something as incongruous. That goes without saying.[6]

An analogy to illustrate this distinction between ordinary judgment and good judgment is that both the hunting guide and the duffer hunter may be walking on the same forest trail, but the experienced guide notices and focuses on things the duffer does not. The hunting guide notices such things as a grass blade springing back from being weighed down by the recent passage of a large animal, the broken twigs, and all the things that enable the guide to form a judgment regarding the proximity of the animal the duffer hunter will adroitly miss with hundreds of rounds from his AK-47. Both the guide and the hunter "see" in some sense the same things. The guide notices things the hunter does not notice. The guide forms judgments the duffer does not.

Of course people with developed taste in any area will not always agree. But if they will talk, they can learn from each other, and may even come to agreement. This may increase their range of appreciation and perhaps sharpen their sense of quality. And, contrary to popular opinion, there is considerable agreement about what is aesthetically good. And what is humorous.

Conclusions

What a tangled web of interrelated issues we have examined and hopefully kept separate and clarified.

We dealt with the issues of the relativity of experiences and judgments in the areas of beauty and incongruity, their "subjectivity" and "relativity," and the confused introduction of "taste" in the discussion, which leads to a fatal equivocation. I suggested that statements of relativity break down into the observation that people do indeed differ with regard to their experiences and judgments. I also suggested that calling something "subjective" does not add much to the discussion, though understanding in what sense something can be subjective does help clarify the situation

I tried to clarify the concept of "taste" in aesthetics and humor by claiming that there is an equivocation on the term, "taste" in many discussions. There are both physical taste and evaluative taste. I suggested we can characterize taste as "developed" or "educated" if we separate the issue of liking something from the issue of knowing or judging that something is good. Educated or developed taste, as differentiated from uneducated or undeveloped taste, can help resolve issues of relativity or subjectivity, or the differences we see in judgments about the quality of a given example or examples in the case of comparisons.

And that, my friends, is about as complicated a set of sentences as I care to write.

Endnotes

[1] The literature on this issue is so extensive and the concepts so completely examined that it would take pages to cite the literature. It could almost be a book in itself. If anyone gets interested enough to pursue the issue, you'll have to do your own research. I intend to save part of a forest by not citing the sources. Besides, I want to keep things as simple as a philosopher can keep things. I do not necessarily accept the philosophical rule: If it's worth doing, it's worth overdoing.

[2] Look where it got him.

[3] Someone said you cannot use "paradigmatically" twice in the same sentence. Poooo. Someone else said you should not use it twice in the same sentence. That makes sense.

[4] Very peccable.

[5] I plead the Fifth on that one.

[6] So please forget I said it.

"I refuse to spend my life worrying about what I eat. There is no pleasure worth forgoing just for an extra three years in a geriatric ward."

John Mortimer

"On the other hand...you have different fingers."

Stephen Wright

Chapter 5
A Sense of Humor

The groundwork has been laid for an explanation of what a sense of humor is, and in this chapter I intend to explain what I think the concept involves.

Before going on with the comparison between the sense of the aesthetic and the sense of humor, which will hopefully illuminate the issue, it is noted that art deals with incongruities in many ways. Humor deals with incongruity in its own, unique way, which is to say, playfully. Much art is imaginative, but not particularly playful. There are exceptions.

Now comes the central comparison, for which you have probably been waiting with baited breath. Incidentally, what do you bait your breath with, and what do you catch? That's an old vaudeville joke. You caught an old vaudeville joke? Extremely awesome!

Please fasten your seat belt before proceeding any further. If you do not have a seat belt, fasten someone else's seatbelt. Just as in the case of the art world, the world of humor has its creators or artists, its works of humor, its consumers or appreciators of humor, and its critics of humor. It also has elements that look like humor but may not be, such as comedy. Seeing humor in this light will help explain what humor is, and that will hopefully throw light on what the sense of humor is.

Admittedly the world of humor is much smaller than the world of art, perhaps because there is more money to be made in art, or what appears to be art, than in humor. There is, of course, money in comedy. Humor is just one aspect of the much larger aesthetic world.

The world of entertainment is the place that real money is made. Pornography is one of the easiest and most lucrative forms of entertainment. It is just a question of uncovering a little talent. Very little talent. Mostly you need to do a whole lot of uncovering.

The humor world depends on the sense of humor just as surely as the aesthetic world depends on the sense of the aesthetic. You have to be in a certain frame of mind to experience either the aesthetic world or the humor world. If humor is simply a kind of aesthetic experience, as I maintain, this conclusion is obvious. However, possession of a sense of the aesthetic does not automatically mean that the person possesses a sense of humor. A sense of humor is more specialized than a sense of the aesthetic since the humorous is a subset or class of the larger category of the aesthetic. People who have a sense of humor also have at least some sense of the aesthetic, but not vice versa.

This is similar to the case in which a person with a great deal of sensitivity to most paintings in general may not have any appreciation at all for a specific kind of painting, such as Contra-Puntalism.

The main difference between a non-humorous aesthetic experience and a humorous experience is that the humorous focuses on incongruities from a playful perspective. Non-humorous aesthetic experiences can focus on a much broader range of phenomena, and they may focus on an incongruity, but not treat it in a humorous way, which is to say a playful way. The non-humorous and the humorous can be combined, of course. Humor can be used as a distraction from the ongoing solemnity of a drama, or it can in and of itself explore the incongruities that are its proper object. Comedy can also lighten up a serious drama when release from the building tension of the plot is required, though comedy does not automatically deal with the playful appreciation of incongruity.

Take a deep breath, and loosen your seat belt. You have it too tight.

The Sense of Humor

The argument gets so complex at this point that I can hardly follow it myself. But it goes like this. Since humor is a response to the incongruous, the sense of humor is the mental capacity to appreciate these incongruous events from a playful perspective. In its strongest form, the sense of humor is the ability to playfully discover or create unexpected and surprising combinations of elements. This ability is usually under more or less conscious control. It needs to be over-emphasized that the sense of humor absolutely requires a playful frame of mind, or playful orientation, regarding an incongruity.

Some experiences are just not likely candidates for humor at a given time, such as in the case of a person being burned at the stake. It takes an extraordinary person to appreciate the incongruities of human life at such a time. A casual observer might be in a little better position to see the humor in the situation, especially if it is presented on a stage by a group of actors and the fire is fake. I am going to avoid any reference to the old song, "There'll be a Hot Time in the Old Town Tonight" at this point. I will grit my teeth and mention, "Light My Fire." Someone has to do it, and I'm not sure I can count on you.

Please recall that laughter and humor are related, but separate. Laughter is not a sure sign that humor is present. Humor may exist in the complete absence of laughter. One of the sources of laughter is incongruity. If an incongruity is produced by someone (a humorist) by pointing out a natural incongruity or creating a purely conceptual incongruity for the purpose of helping us appreciate its qualities, and if the appreciator is in a playful frame of mind, then we have humor.

Comics sometimes use techniques other than humor to get laughs, so comedy and humor are separate, though related. Comedy has many dimensions, some involving questionable moral tactics such as the excessive use of profanity or ridicule, or the infliction of physical pain. Laugh tracks are of questionable morality also. These often will get laughs, and laughs are the goal of comedy, but merely getting laughs is not the goal of humor. One can also ridicule or disgust by using humor, though these are not the purpose of humor.

Attitudes

Let's continue with a definition of a key term. A sense of humor is an attitude or set of attitudes that involve a tendency to notice, explore, and sometimes create incongruities, and to appreciate them in a playful way that is usually pleasurable. Since the term "attitude' is crucial here, let's put some effort into defining it.

An attitude is a habitual psychological structure that influences and often controls what we perceive, that is, what we think and feel, and the beliefs we have about those things we perceive and feel. Though the term "attitude" has, in common usage, come to mean mostly a bad or hostile attitude, I am using the term much more generally. Roughly, an attitude is a set of habits with which we approach life, and many attitudes are learned early in life.

To take a simple example, a person might have an optimistic attitude, or a pessimistic attitude. The optimist thinks, feels, and believes that life is worthwhile, that good will often prevail and efforts to produce it will often be realized. An optimist may overlook or simply not notice the more negative aspects of life, or minimize their negativity. He selectively sees mostly the positive things around him. Not so for the pessimist, who has the opposite patterns of thought, feeling, and belief. Such a person might have an angry attitude, expecting things around him to frustrate him and tending to lash out either verbally or physically at those frustrating objects or situations. We all have a collection of attitudes that operate in certain situations. We usually have some major attitudes that are operative for most periods of our life. Optimism and pessimism are examples of major attitudes.

It's a cliché that the optimist sees the glass as half full, and the pessimist sees it as half empty. Perhaps the realist empties the glass and pours himself another. Perhaps realism is the attitude that is neither optimistic nor pessimistic, but simply takes life as it comes, with fewer expectations and an open mind. Just off hand, a sense of realism would seem to work well with a sense of humor. A realist may see much more of life and its potential for humor because he sees but does not overemphasize both the positive and the negative.

Now back to the sense of humor. The sense of humor involves intellectual play. It may be engaged by noticing a surprising incongruity in our physical world, or it may respond to someone's conscious attempt to point out an incongruity to us in a playful manner. It may even create a new incongruity, usually on the conceptual level, though not always.

Visual and auditory incongruities often occur, or can be created if we choose. The sense of humor may respond to a random occurrence in our world, such as a person slipping on a banana peel (an ancient cliché from our primate ancestors), or in elaborate word and conceptual play that requires considerable effort to follow. A musical composition may be intentionally put together involving musical clichés, or sounds and combinations of sounds not ordinarily heard in music. There are many possibilities, most probably not yet explored. What the world really needs now are explorers on the frontiers of incongruity.

For example, "Time heals all wounds" is a cliché. We all know it and say it, even if it's not true. "Time wounds all heels" is a fresh, incongruous inversion of the cliché, and is humorous. If the inversion is used so often that it loses most of its meaning, it too can become a cliché, and new ways must be found to point out this rather central incongruity in our world, which is that both the good and the bad are subject to the ravages of Father Time, and those ravages give life its poignancy, its paradoxes, and its profundity. That sounded almost philosophical. Sorry, once in a while I have to do that to avoid going to sleep.

Incongruities whether discovered or created may be visual, auditory, tactile, olfactory, and I suppose even gastronomical, though the latter three are probably not all that common. An example of an olfactory incongruity would be a skunk that smelled like a rose bush. A gastronomical incongruity would be an exotic meat, perhaps dromedary meat that does not taste like chicken.

The overall experience that results from the engagement of the sense of humor is usually one of pleasure in the widest sense. It may be a delight in the unexpectedness of the stimulus, or in the ability of the humorist to point out what had not been noticed before. There is, after all, a difference between saying funny things and saying things funny.

Holy Hemorrhoids, Batman! What an explosion in a word factory.

Appreciation

It is necessary to appreciate appreciation if we are to understand the sense of humor. Though we are dealing with a noun, it would be wiser to switch to the verb form, "to appreciate," to make clear that appreciating is an act done by an active mind and not an inert pile of postulation which can only be located by a philosophical GPS. For the sake of a definition of the sense of humor, we are using the noun form. It is shorter that way, and looks better on the page.

The meaning of the term "to appreciate" is complex. There is an economic sense of "to appreciate" which means to increase in economic value. This can often be precisely measured. We are not concerned with that meaning.

There is a cluster of evaluative senses of our verb, as seen in such uses as "I appreciate the sunset," "I appreciate your problem with your mother," "I don't usually appreciate the bombast of Wagner," and "I can see you appreciate the incongruity involved with the idea of space aliens kidnapping one of our bad girl starlets and holding her for ransom. How much would we demand they pay us for us to take her back?" How much would we offer to try to get them to keep her?

We are not dealing with the issue of simply liking something. We can appreciate something without liking it. I might appreciate the majestic force of a volcano and not like the fact that the lava is going to soon overflow my community. Likewise, I can like something without appreciating it. I may like *The Three Stooges* but realize it is not particularly good humor. I also may not appreciate the fact that their humor appeals mostly to children and the "young" in mind. That says too much about me.

The act of appreciating involves recognizing the worth of something. It involves the discovery or creation of value. You have to have some sort of knowledge in order to appreciate something. That also distinguishes it from cases of simple liking. You can like something without recognizing its worth or value. You can value something without liking it. The recognition of value or worth involves the possession of some kind of knowledge other than that involved with liking.

The knowledge involved in appreciating usually is knowledge of the objects or situation in question. People who have had trouble with their mother are in a position to appreciate mother trouble much more completely and profoundly than someone who hasn't had that sort of problem.

The kind of appreciation involved in exercising a sense of humor is very close to the kind of appreciation involved in experiencing art. It is evaluative, it involves the possession of relevant knowledge, and it works independently of liking.

Origins of a Sense of Humor

Another important question is where the sense of humor comes from. The answer is closely related to the question of where the sense of the aesthetic comes from. Our comparison strikes again!

Kids play, often in delight or amusement. We take their sense of delight and try to enhance it by calling attention to the sights, sounds, and tactile sensations of their world. We try to develop a sense of the beautiful in them. We try to help them understand and delight in their world. Likewise we try to teach them what is funny or incites laughter, to build on this sense of play. We laugh with them. Then when they are almost old enough, we get really serious with most of them, and encourage them to stop playing, for there are serious things to do in this world, and play interferes with them. Wisely, they mostly ignore us. Nevertheless, we insist that it is time to put the weight of the world on their shoulders and put their noses to the grindstone. Tough on noses, but not so much on grindstones.

We are right, of course. Children need to get serious, since life is said to be in large part serious business, and you cannot play forever. Or so we say. They were developing the sense of the funny, which is a precursor of a sense of humor. The sense of the funny is a skill at determining where a person is likely to find the amusing, rather than simply waiting for something to happen which causes laughs. It also includes a habitual understanding of when it is appropriate to laugh and when it is not. Social laughter, laughter at the appropriate time, and the avoidance of laugher at an improper time, is an important element in the personality of most people.

In developing the sense of the funny no further, we impoverish the lives of children and adults, depriving them of a source of delight, and perhaps depriving them of a tool for coping with the pains, the disappointments, and the frustrations that life presents us. To become the sense of humor, the sense of the funny must become habitual, and must go beyond response to the merely comedic. An attitude involving the development of appreciation of incongruities must occur.

When does the sense of the funny become the sense of humor? It varies in individual cases. We hone the ability to laugh at the proper times. From this proceeds the ability to appreciate the incongruities of life. It takes more learning for a person to have a sense of humor than to learn to laugh when others laugh, to laugh when someone says something that is called "funny" and we feel obliged to laugh. It takes less work to laugh at the stimulus of a laugh track. Most of these activities involve little learning.

Just as in the case of the sense of the aesthetic, we often abandon the development of the sense of humor at a certain point. We provide children with the shallow material of the entertainment industry, and we provide laugh tracks or prepared audiences to help them know what is "funny." Of course most of this comedic material is used for our economic exploitation, but we are Americans, and it is our inalienable right and our destiny to be economically exploited.

When people are discouraged from developing their sense of the funny, we deprive them of discovering the power of humor. We may deprive them of a sense of humor. We give them the easy way out. We teach them to laugh when they are supposed to, and only when they are supposed to. We fill their lives with the comedic equivalent of purple velvet Elvises, and rarely tell them there is more, and better. We give them sitcoms with laugh tracks, and maybe that is enough to get through life. But is it enough to enhance life?

Laughter has certain benefits, though if you expect it to cure serious disease you'll probably be disappointed. But if you know it might help deal with serious situations, including disease, you are ahead of the game. If you have used laughter to deal with pain, and developed a habit of doing this, you are to be commended. If you have learned to use humor, or just the comedic, to do this, you may be benefiting the people around you as well as yourself.

We can use a sense of humor throughout the day. We are presented with numerous incongruities. Some are simply frustrating. Others we ignore. But if our sense of humor becomes strong, and we adopt it as an important way of dealing with our world, it can be a source of goodness for ourselves and the people around us. Just how a sense of humor is beneficial will be discussed in the following chapter.

What a Sense of Humor is Not

It may be helpful to indicate what the sense of humor is not. The sense of humor is not the ability to laugh when other people laugh just because you hear their laughter. That response is contact laughter, and seems to be built into our genetic inheritance by generations of social laughers. However, laughter may indicate a person has attained a sense of humor.

The implication of my point is that someone who laughs

long and loud, longer and louder indeed than most, does not necessarily possess any sense of humor. Almost everyone laughs when the crowd is laughing. Perhaps a person with a sense of humor can be caught laughing when no one else is. And he can often explain why he is laughing. Nevertheless he may be considered a bit strange. Or more than a bit strange.

The sense of humor is not required in order to respond to something that someone labels a joke. Responding to jokes is often a social ritual. The joke is told and everyone laughs. In many cases everyone feels a little more comfortable, and life goes on. Good jokes and bad jokes seem to be equally good at soliciting laughter, with the exception of puns. We groan at puns. Can groaning be a type of laughter? If the groaning indicates genuine pain, maybe certain forms of pain also encourage group solidarity. Almost any kind of shared experience seems to contribute to a feeling of group cohesion.

Conclusion

Let's put it all together. The sense of humor is an attitude that playfully notices incongruities and appreciates them. A person with a sense of humor habitually looks for the incongruities in life and playfully explores them. A person with a sense of the aesthetic also deals with incongruities, but usually not in a playful manner. A sense of humor is a specific form of a sense of the aesthetic.

Comedy is different from humor, though the two can mix. The goal of comedy is laughter. The goal of humor is playful appreciation of an incongruity.

Children are encouraged to develop a sense of laughter. This is the ability to discern when to laugh. It is a preliminary step to a sense of humor.

The sense of humor is a learned response, much like the aesthetic response. Of course that which can be learned can often be taught. It's as simple and as complex as that.

Endnotes

There are no endnotes to Chapter 5. That's just the way it worked out. You don't really need endnotes on all chapters. The lack of endnotes does not violate any fish and game laws. Besides, not having endnotes for every chapter helps neutralize the nasty habit of having endnotes for every chapter.

Chapter 5: A Sense of Humor

"Truth is often stranger than fiction because fiction is obliged to make sense."

Mark Twain

"The problem with political jokes is they get elected."

Henry Cate

Chapter 6

The Role and Value of Humor

Some extravagant claims have been made to answer the question of the value of humor. Putting aside for the next chapter the nearly impossible question of the connection between humor and happiness, let's reflect on some issues.

Let's examine the pedigrees of comedy and humor, as well as the differences between the two. This can provide some insights into the value of humor and of comedy. There are significant similarities between the two, and some important differences.

Comedy and Humor

Let me sharpen the distinction between comedy and humor. Comedy is the attempt to produce laughter. Almost any kind of laughter will do. Humor is the playful appreciation of incongruity, which is to say the unexpected, the paradoxical, the illogical, and in general the often surprising elements in human existence. Laughter is not the goal of humor; appreciation of incongruity is. This is not to say that humor cannot involve laughter. It often does, but it need not.

Comedy is intended to be amusement. As amusement, it can take us away from some of the practical and sometimes darker aspects of our lives, at least temporarily, and as such provides some relief from the sometimes messy business of living. Comedy is not unique in this, however. Humor can do this also.

There are many other forms of diversion or amusement. Sleep can take us away, temporarily, from the problems of life. So can drugs. Death takes us permanently away from our problems, and this obvious observation has been a strong motivating factor in the behavior of some people. People climb mountains, attend sporting events, start affairs, get drunk, get married, massage their electronic devices, and find many other ways to escape the pressure of living for shorter or longer periods of time. The pressure of living can include boredom as well as distress at the complexity of life.

Humor can be an amusing diversion, but it can do more. It has the serious task of helping us explore the incongruities in our lives rather than simply escaping them temporarily. The amusement factor is secondary in humor.

More importantly, humor is a form of aesthetic experience, and comedy is not. As aesthetic experience humor possesses the general characteristics of aesthetic experience. One of these characteristics is that we can learn more about our world and ourselves as a consequence of our aesthetic experience.

The visual arts (painting, sculpture and related arts) can make us more aware of the sensory qualities of our world. The visual arts may also employ symbolism to show us something about our world and ourselves. The same goes for the musical arts. Drama reveals truths about the quality of human experience, especially with regard to our dealings with each other. Architecture, while more utilitarian, can make us appreciative of our physical environment, the volumes and shapes, the quality of light between and among objects, and other factors of this sort. The literary arts can explore the richness of human experience in many ways. Poets can make us aware of the expressiveness of our language, and give us insight into their world.

This is, of course, only a partial listing.

The Fine Arts and the Utilitarian Arts

The connection between the fine arts and the utilitarian arts needs to be clarified if we are to understand more about the nature of humor and its connection with comedy.

Let's consider some examples from the graphic arts that are intended primarily or entirely for utilitarian purposes, such as advertising. I have in mind the use of logos with which companies and other artificial persons identify themselves. The logos may be attractive. They are rarely art because they teach us little or nothing about the things art enlightens us about. They may perform a number of functions, but dealing with the quality of human experience is usually not one of them. This is true for most examples of advertising, though of course there are formal principles that apply to the production of advertising. Once in a while some examples of advertising escape these limits and become art in the higher sense.

Advertising is usually not art in the full sense of the word, though we do derivatively use the term "art" to designate anything done with skill in accord with certain agreed upon principles of excellence in execution. These are utilitarian or practical arts, which means only that they involve the exercise of skill. Much photography fits into this category, though it can rise to the status of fine art. Pictures of little Ralphie kissing his baby sister may have considerable emotional appeal in some circles, but they aren't the *Mona Lisa* by any stretch. Come to think of it, nothing is the *Mona Lisa* except the *Mona Lisa*, and it has perhaps ceased to be an art object, being now an icon. Or a cliché.

The gulf between comedy and humor is the same as the gulf between the practical or utilitarian arts on the one hand, and the fine arts on the other. In any given instance, the line between the two categories, in either the case of fine arts or the case of humor, may be hard to draw. This is common in our complex world. But there are enough clear and non-debatable examples of practical arts on the one hand, and fine arts on the other, or between comedy on one hand and humor on the other. In a few words, intended function separates the two sets.

This is not to deny that perfectly reasonable discussion can be launched and perhaps never terminated with regard to whether one specific example, for instance Monty Python's film, *The Meaning of Life*, is humor, comedy, or perhaps a mixture of both.

Another way to understand this relationship between comedy and humor is to note that comedy can succeed purely on the basis of a good laugh track and the reality of contact laughter. No sense of humor is needed to have a great time with comedy, though it is helpful. The production of laughter is the goal, and in successful comedy, laughter is produced. To appreciate humor one needs a fairly well developed sense of humor in addition to the traits necessary to experience comedy.

Since the experience of humor is one type of the experience of the fine arts, humor can give us insight into the ambiguities and incongruities in life. It can lay bare the sophistic core of politics, as Will Rogers and Mark Twain did. It can explore our attitudes toward death, as some of the epitaphs on gravestones do. It can catch us in the inconsistencies in our own beliefs, as some of the minority comedians do. Comedy can certainly employ humor, and vice versa. They combine rather well to make it more pleasant to hear the messages we sometimes find hard to hear.

Value of Laughter

It is past time to give an orderly, general presentation of the value of laughter and of humor, now that the distinction between comedy and humor has been clarified. Let's more closely examine what laughter and comedy can do, and then what humor can do in addition.

Laughter, no matter what its source, is claimed to be a social lubricant. It can smooth our daily relationships with each other. It usually indicates friendly intent, a non-hostile attitude, and an acceptance of the people around us. This seems to be one of laughter's primary functions. Humor and comedy, of course, can do this also.

Laughter has many other purposes, one of which is ridicule. It may still build relationships among those who are not the victims of this laughter. There are yet other forms of laughter, such as drug-induced laughter or the laughter of nervousness, that simply do not have relevance to this discussion. We are focusing on what might be called "happy laughter," that is, laughter that does not involve negative or destructive mental content. Judging laughter to be happy requires experience and an appreciation of the context.

The topic of social cohesiveness certainly needs to be considered further. Laughter can build a sense of community, of purpose, of group solidarity. Laughter helps us feel psychologically closer to friends and even strangers. We can celebrate the positive events and get through the negative events when we feel even a superficial closeness to others. In times of tragedy a shared laugh can help people feel less overwhelmed and alone. Many people who survived concentration camps report that even small, daily doses of laughter in almost overwhelmingly difficult circumstances helped get them through.

There is, however, a dark side to the social cohesiveness produced by laughter, or any of the other social glues we use, such as shared beliefs. A group can be solidified by laughter, but the group may turn laughter, in the form of ridicule, toward other individuals or groups. In other words, the in-group not only solidifies itself through laughter, but also increases that cohesiveness by ridicule of an out-group or two.

The out-group, of course, may send the ridicule back in another form if the out-group is sufficiently large or strong. What goes around may indeed often come around. Is that what that expression means?

Ridicule can lead to violence. "Disrespect" is a form of ridicule. That is no laughing matter. For example, you can't keep putting religious symbols into vessels of urine without some problems. Or making fun of Muhammad. He may be dead, but many of his disciples are not. Demagogues seem to intuitively understand the power of ridicule and hate, which seems to be stronger than the power of love. People can surrender any sense of responsibility they may have to the group or the demagogue.

Another positive value of laughter is that a person

who laughs easily is often trusted more than a critical, nagging person. Being trusted rather than avoided can have a positive effect on the person who laughs easily. The downside is that easy laughter can be faked.

Those of you who want to comment on the present world situation should feel free to do so. All I am going to say is that religions that profess to practice love as their primary principle have used hate all too often as a strong motivational tool. Love apparently produces good feelings, but hate produces results. Incongruity strikes again. Don't you just hate that?

Laughter can produce relaxation, and reduce frustration and anger. So can humor. Humor especially may elevate us from negative mental states by refocusing the mind. This is of course true of many kinds of diversion, and not just laughter and humor. Certainly diversion from our problems is periodically a desirable thing, and can allow us to return to our problems with different and perhaps more productive feelings. Even the use of ridicule can make something appear less threatening. The use of ridicule with regard to death is a theme found within and outside of art.

Our friends in psychology warn us that laughter as diversion has some hazards. People may use laughter as a way not only to temporarily relieve the negative feelings accompanying a problem, but also may use it so effectively that they never get around to dealing with the problem. They "laugh it off." They don't take the situation as a serious problem, never facing the consequences until the consequences are dire. Or worse. In this case, rather than helping solve problems, laughter makes the problem worse.

Some thinkers, such as Freud as you may recall from our earlier discussion, have emphasized the ability of laughter to provide relief from the tensions involved in conforming our behavior to the demands of society, especially with regard to our sexual and aggressive tendencies. This may include relief from conforming to anything society dictates. Relief from the bonds of conformity is not to be laughed at. Or maybe it is. And perhaps laughter, even the laughter of ridicule, is a way to relieve our aggressive tendencies in a relatively safe way, at least as compared with using thermonuclear devices on things and people that persistently frustrate us.

The Value of Humor

The above are a few of the claims that have been made regarding the value of laughter. Certainly all of them apply to the question of the value of humor, as we have noted. In addition, on behalf of humor, it can be argued that the playful exploration of incongruities may help us understand the incongruities in our situation more thoroughly. This may help us see alternative ways of dealing with our problems. If we see the incongruous elements, perhaps we can put them together in ways that suggest solutions to our present problems.

There may be an even greater benefit to humor. The German philosopher Friedrich Nietzsche (1844-1900) claimed that art in the form of tragic drama has the power to allow us to face the most difficult truths of human existence, such as its apparent meaninglessness, painfulness, and its abrupt termination in the apparent finality of death.[1] I am suggesting we acknowledge the ability of humor to do this also, and to do it better than laughter alone. Such an addition is logical if my contention that humor is a form of art is correct.

Since one of our most difficult truths is the fact of our own mortality, we would expect that death should be one of the important topics for humor. Humor can help us see death in a new and perhaps more insightful way, and reconcile us to the fact that one day we will wake up dead. Or maybe not.

It has been said that creativity consists in the ability to put ideas together in new ways. That is precisely what humor attempts to do, and on occasion, succeeds in doing, even with regard to death. Aside from that, we can put the elements of our lives together in new combinations, and these combinations may provide the fresh perspectives to make our decisions more effective and our problems less daunting, even if not completely solvable.

If nothing else, putting the elements of a boring situation together in new ways can make the situation less boring. A lecture can become almost riveting if a member of the audience decides to count how many times the lecturer says "like" when "approximately" is meant. Or when silence needs to be filled, in the estimation of the speaker. It is, like, a common practice like, one like I don't personally like, like.[2]

It has been claimed that people with a sense of humor are happier, more creative, brighter, have more friends and live healthier lives. This claim will be explored in a later chapter. There is some support for such claims other than prejudice, but there is no universal agreement, partly because the question of what a sense of humor is has not been decided. That is what this book is trying to do. Remember the mantra: Laughter is not a reliable sign of a sense of humor any more than it is a reliable sign of a sense of the sadistic. But in reality that's a little long for a mantra.

What does seem fairly clear, at least to the mental health professions, is that people who cannot laugh at all most likely have some serious problems they have not yet dealt with effectively. Those who laugh most of the time most likely are in the same condition.

On the other hand, the emerging ability to laugh at a situation often means that we are approaching part of life differently. When a client can laugh at some of his problems, many therapists take that as a sign that improvement is occurring. Plus, the ability to create comedy and humor gives us a kind of power, which is the power to confront our problems and not passively react to them or blindly accept them.

Perhaps even on the way to the gallows we can exercise some control if we can see the humor in the situation, or at least see that there is something laughable if not completely humorous. The laughter may be nervous laughter in such a case. Perhaps laughter in this situation will help us realize that we will be rid of all our hang-ups when we get hung up. As one humorist remarked, bacon's not the only thing that's cured by hanging from a string.

Humor and Objectivity

It has been claimed that humor can give us a type of objectivity. In order to evaluate this claim, we need to understand what objectivity is.

The paradigm of objectivity is the scientist, peering at his experiment with dispassionate eyes. This paradigm is also the paradigm of silliness, and it's a shame it ever appeared. Scientists are often, if not always, passionate about their work. If they weren't, they wouldn't do it unless the pay was extraordinarily good. Science is not successful because it is dispassionate. Science is successful to the extent that it prevents passion from influencing its judgments.

People are passionate beings, and that is good. Passion has an important place in our world. Unfortunately it can cloud judgment and lead to false conclusions and unfortunate actions. The goal is not to obliterate passion, which is probably not possible, even if it were desirable. The job is to find a way to keep passion from excessively influencing or determining the judgments of science, and also many of the crucial, non-scientific decisions we have to make in our everyday lives.

A sense of humor can give objectivity in the sense of relative freedom from the influence of passion. We can laugh at what had previously been taken too seriously. This may not endear us to people who still take the situation as completely serious. Such laughter may be the sign that we have a new perspective or set of perspectives from which to view our world. It can free us from the grip of a given passion, or liberate us from an especially problematical orientation, which may be as simple as an excessively practical orientation toward life.

One further point needs to be added to our account of the value of humor. In a situation in which powerful feelings are involved on the part of some individuals, the light touch of humor may defuse the situation a bit and allow an over-stressed person to hear a message that needs to be considered.

Perhaps the use of humor in education can make difficult and potentially boring material interesting. A speaker who can make things light and funny may be more effective than someone who preaches, shouts, rants, raves, browbeats, or gets too deadly serious. Or who induces terminal boredom in his listeners.

A person who can soften the impact of a tragedy by lightening the scene with thoughtful and sensitive humor may add more to the quality of a human life than all the actions of politicians or religious figures. In using humor in these situations, a great deal of sensitivity is required since raw feelings are exposed and humor might be seen as a lack of respect.

Humor and Serious Diseases

As a final note before closing this chapter, it should be observed that so far the claim that laughter and humor can help cure serious diseases has not been substantiated by careful investigation. The meager scientific investigation that has been done does not seem to support the contention. Laughter may not be the best medicine for dealing with serious physical conditions, but it can be helpful. If you have cancer, trust in laughter and humor by all means, but see a good oncologist. If the oncologist gives you little hope, you're really going to need not only a massive dose of laughter from any source, but also perhaps a sense of humor. You can call it psychological chicken soup. I wouldn't.

Conclusions

In this chapter I have attempted to state some contributions to human life that entertainment, and especially comedy, make. One of these is to divert us from our problems for a while, with one result being that our dark moods are lifted a bit so we return to the task of dealing with our problems with renewed energy. This is in addition to the social value of cementing group solidarity and in many cases promoting trust among people.

Since a sense of humor is a subset of a sense of the aesthetic, humor in addition can accomplish what fine art can accomplish, which is to present an alternative perspective on our world, or to point out something we had not noticed. So in addition to renewal of energy, and freedom for a time from our pressing problems, we may have new tools to deal with the problems as a consequence of exercising our sense of humor. In some cases we may only be able to accept those parts of the problem we cannot change, and that acceptance may be made easier by the recognition that things may not be as bad as we had feared, which is a new perspective in itself. In the broader context we may appreciate our own incongruities better, and understand that we, and our problems, are not as important as we had thought. We may not have gotten over ourselves, but we may have at least caught up with ourselves.

When a person discovers that he is not the real center of the universe, he can vacate that position so that someone else may assume it. The center of the universe is not so big that we can all occupy it. It is usually a lonely place, best avoided if at all possible. Its rewards are transitory and are usually damaging to everyone in the general vicinity.

Endnotes

[1] Most any version of Nietzsche's book, *The Birth of Tragedy from the Spirit of Music* will serve as a source for this part of Nietzsche's thinking.

[2] If you think that last sentence in the chapter needs more commas, be my guest. Use your own comma shaker, however.

Chapter 6: The Role and Value of Humor

"What this country needs is more unemployed politicians."

Edward Langley

"Right now I'm having amnesia and déjà vu at the same time. I think I've forgotten this before."

Stephen Wright

"We Jews believe it was Santa Claus who killed Jesus Christ."

Richard "Kinky" Friedman

Chapter 7

Humor and Happiness

Only a fool or a philosopher writes a chapter on happiness and humor. Only a person with a well developed sense of humor reads it. If you have gotten this far, you probably have a well developed sense of humor. So here is what the fool has to say about happiness and humor.

Old Aristotle used to say that you should expect no more clarity than the subject matter will allow. The following thoughts will hopefully have some clarity. With that caveat for whatever emptors we can find, we're off like a herd of turtles. Or is that a flock? Anyway, let's get the flock out of here.

Happiness

Those who seriously consider the topic of happiness are forced to decide whether what the term "happiness" denotes is a short-term or a long-term condition. What this boils down to is deciding whether happiness is an emotion on the one hand, or a condition that lasts longer and is less subject to rapid change on the other.

To resolve this issue briefly so we can get on with other confusions, I will simply state there are two kinds of happiness: A short-term feeling as denoted in such statements as "I was very happy today to see my old friend Bob." The other sense of happiness denotes a long-term condition, as when we say, "She has lived a happy life." Such a life is consistent with short-term negative emotions and physical suffering. There are happy people who live through great tragedies or live with ongoing pain. There are also unhappy people who, though they have everything going for them, seem from

101

all their words and actions to be absolutely and abjectly miserable. They sometimes verify our judgment by killing themselves.

The fact that laughter is connected to some of the positive emotions, perhaps those that can be called "happy," is no longer a governmental secret. The assertion has been declassified. However, any attempt to construct long-term happiness from short-term positive feelings doesn't seem to work. Happiness for a man does not consist of marriage to a deaf, mute nymphomaniac who owns a liquor store. Happiness for a woman does not consist of marriage to a handsome money-machine so devoid of personal interests and goals that he has time only for her. There are, of course, always a significant number of volunteers who will try some variation on these approaches for themselves. Fantasies die hard.

It is evident that happiness is not a continuing positive frame of mind, much less a life of successive pleasures uninterrupted by any feelings less than positive. It also seems evident that happiness does involve successive positive emotions of various sorts, interrupted and perhaps accompanied by the stresses of life.

When the bubbles in the champagne glass of life are encountered, there are various ways to deal with them. People can ignore a problem, at least temporarily, and maybe for a long period of time. People can deny the existence of a problem or minimize it. People can face a problem head on and deal with it. People may not resolve their difficulties but may learn to live with them. In some extreme cases, people commit suicide. The latter move seems to solve all problems for the person committing suicide, but not for the people remaining alive. Someone has to dispose of the carcass.

Problems rarely vanish or solve themselves, though of course a few do. When you look at genuinely happy people, people who are happy long term, they don't restrict themselves to ignoring, denying, or minimizing problems. They usually deal with them in a variety of creative, effective ways.

The important kind of happiness for our purposes is long-term. This kind of happiness depends on a set of attitudes as well as on skills involved in dealing with the world effectively. It also involves appreciation of one's place and role in that world. It includes gratitude for many things, quite a few of which are beyond our control most of the time. For example, we don't choose to be born. We don't choose to come into the world at this particular time and in this particular civilization. But here we are, and for many of us, especially people in western culture, the potential for happiness is pretty high. The world could always be better, but happy people appreciate their lives and the world they have, just as they are. Of course many of us would like to improve our world, and leave it a bit better than when we came into it.

It is important to have skills in order to deal with the frustrations, disappointments, and failures of everyday living, as well as skills involved with avoiding these conditions. A happy person has learned many of these skills, some because they were taught to him, and some because he used his intelligence to figure out what was going wrong with his life, and how to fix or avoid those problems. He probably sought and got good advice from other people. He may have simply imitated happy people for a while until he developed the habits.

A number of people helped make this physical world, and our personal world, a pretty good place. We live on the material level better than medieval royalty. We know enough of our physical world to have conquered many diseases and extended our life spans to the point we can become really decrepit. We know enough to be confused about the nature of our universe and our place in it, though we have usually achieved some sort of meaning and explanation for it that satisfies us. All these aspects, and many more, are experienced with a sense of gratitude by a happy person.

We can safely say that a happy person has made sense of her world. We need to add that there is no one correct sense to be made of the world, though there seem to be many senses that guarantee that a person will not be happy. Each person has to make sense of the world in terms of her own experience, in terms of the range of ideas she has learned about her world, and in terms of as much honesty as she can muster. On the other hand, a person can accept a ready-made explanation of what the world is about, much as a ready-made garment can be purchased off the rack at a clothing store. The world nevertheless is as it is, whether we want it to be that way or not. Self-deception is not a good anchor for happiness, though there may be a place for small amounts of it. Self-deception is a human being's spiritual shadow. That almost sounded philosophical. I slip up now and then. I wish I understood it.

In addition, a relative freedom from want is important. It is hard to be happy though starving to death, or being the guest of honor at a banquet of cannibals. That does give new meaning to the old suggestion of having a friend for lunch, or the comment that Joe is one tough guy.

Happiness also involves making peace with those negative conditions we are never quite able to bury or change. It involves putting our life in perspective. It also involves knowing how to continue to play. We start life by playing. We need to keep that sense of play for a lifetime, though the manners of expression may change as time goes along.

Happiness is not an all or nothing condition; there are degrees of happiness. Some people are, over time, happier than others. Some periods of a person's life are happier than others. The bifurcation between the happy and the unhappy is a device for attaining some simplicity in a complex situation, at the risk of oversimplification.

Who is to say which people are happy? One obvious answer is that the person himself is the best judge of his or her happiness, though self-deception and intellectual confusion about what happiness is make this a big undertaking. On the other hand, a perceptive outsider can occasionally judge more clearly than the person himself regarding the quality of the life. The outsider may have an objectivity or perspective we can rarely attain by ourselves. That outsider might be willing to communicate some observations. One guideline a person can use to judge his own life was suggested by the philosopher Friedrich Nietzsche: Would you live your life over, exactly as it has been, mistakes, disasters, and all? It's hard to give a cheap answer to such an expensive question.

Our goal is to understand how a sense of humor could contribute to making a life happier, though a sense of humor would not be the sole determining factor. There is much more to it. I told you this wouldn't be simple. This is not a book on happiness. If it were, it would be no laughing matter. Or maybe it would.

105

The factors listed in the previous paragraphs are not all necessary, but quite a few of them have to be present, or a life is not a particularly happy one. Maybe a life lacking in most of the conditions is not a happy life, or perhaps it is an existence involving what Thoreau called "quiet desperation." There is an overabundance of types of lives, but many of them are not particularly happy. Perhaps happiness is rare in the human species. There is certainly data to suggest that belief.

So how do laughter and humor fit into all this?[1]

A Sense of Humor

We investigated the various functions of laughter in a previous chapter. Laughter can be a valuable distraction, of a temporary sort, from "the slings and arrows of outrageous fortune," as one Brit put it. Providing smooth social interactions and group solidarity is another. In virtually all cases, laughter by itself is only a temporary and superficial distraction from the problems of being human.

One of the primary problems in our advanced and somewhat civilized society is boredom. Most jobs involve a great deal of routine, repetitive behavior. Wars are fought, affairs are consummated, perhaps murders are committed at least partially for the sake of avoiding or alleviating boredom. Laughter is one of the ways to avoid or relieve boredom. It is a temporary solution, but then, most solutions to most problems are relatively temporary. The permanent solution is death. It cures a host of problems. But as a solution it has its downside.

However, I am interested in the contribution of humor, not laughter. More specifically, I am interested in whether a sense of humor can help make a human existence happy, or a happy life happier, since happiness involves degrees. Laughter can produce a temporary, short-term "happy" feeling as well as express it. Some people call this feeling "mirth." Comedy seeks the short-term laugh, hopefully accompanied by mirth.

A sense of humor involves a habitual use of the intellect and so is likely to have more long-term effects. Laughter, on the other hand, does not necessarily involve any thought at all, as mentioned earlier. People may laugh out of feelings of superiority, because of suppressed needs, or from nervousness. Nervous laughter can become a personality trait, to the detriment of the person having that trait. Laughter has its place, and can be a wonderful temporary state, but it may involve no thought at all, and it may or may not accompany the feeling of mirth.

A sense of humor is not essentially involved with laughter, though a person with a sense of humor usually laughs or at least smiles occasionally, and sees some of what is funny in our world, including herself. She is comfortable with quite a few of the incongruities in her life, and appreciates at least some of them. There may nevertheless be more incongruities than appreciators. Many appreciators deal with the same incongruities that other appreciators deal with. Some incongruities are very hard to ignore. By now you might be eager to find out which ones those are. The next chapter will deal with some of them.

Appreciation

Appreciation is such an important concept in this inquiry that I will spend a few more paragraphs explaining it, just to build on what was said earlier. We say such things as "I appreciate that sunset. It's gorgeous." "I appreciate the way that home is laid out. It's so sensible, so informal, and the views into the garden are great." "I appreciate your problem, my friend, for I have been there too."

Looking at these various statements, we can conclude that appreciation involves understanding something or knowing quite a bit about that subject or situation, seeing its role in our world or the world of someone else, and having a positive orientation toward it, even if the object or situation in itself is negative. If people are involved, empathy almost always plays a role in appreciation. We can appreciate the feelings of another person who has lost a loved one, especially if we have experienced a similar event. We can appreciate both the positives and negatives in life. The positives are the easiest to appreciate. The negatives are mostly overrated as objects of appreciation.

One of the reasons children are incapable of happiness, though they can laugh, play and enjoy life, is because they do not have enough experience to be able to appreciate anyone's existence, including their own.

That is enough for now to help us appreciate appreciation.

Of course this is vague, but we have Aristotle reminding us that we should expect no more clarity than the subject matter will allow. And with that I cop out and get to a treatment of humor, a sense of humor, and its impact on our long-term happiness.

A Developed Sense of Humor

Most people assume they have at minimum a magnificent sense of humor. Many people also think they can appreciate great art, as found in the typical soap opera or hanging in a discount store. Many people judge they have a wonderful sense of humor because they laugh fairly often. Sometimes they even tell a joke. They are sure they have a great aesthetic sense because they can appreciate a picture of a baby or cry during a soap opera.

We suggested a couple of paragraphs ago that laughter can be trivial or even meaningless. The hollow laugh of the mad man is a staple in bad movies. Many people are reassured they have a superb sense of humor because they laugh at what other people laugh at. "Laugh and the world laughs with you..." We need to reconsider the fact that contact laughter may have very little understanding behind it.

A developed sense of humor is as uncommon as a developed sense of the aesthetic. Many of us are on the road to developing and improving both, but it takes years. Both senses are creative traits, and we are aided by those people whose creativity has made our world so much better. Our artists and humorists are at least as valuable as our inventors and engineers.

The value of people who can produce laughter is obvious, but the question is that of the contribution of the possession of a sense of humor to the quality of an individual existence. To keep the issue as clear as possible, consider my definition of a sense of humor. A sense of humor is a tendency, habit, or disposition to playfully appreciate some of the incongruities with which our existence is so copiously endowed. We are occasionally able to appreciate some of both the positive and negative incongruities in life. But just what does this question of the connection between happiness and a sense of humor involve? What a good question! I am glad that I asked it, because at this point it is exactly the question that ought to be raised.

We are almost constantly making practical decisions, some relatively important and some trivial. We often make these decisions habitually. For example, we avoid walking into trees without thinking about it. We drive our cars habitually, not thinking about the location of the brake or the accelerator pedal, though a question like this might have been of crucial importance when we were learning how to drive.

Being practical in this sense serves us well. One of the ways in which this practical attention serves us is in simple perception. We recognize a tree without difficulty. We see that our present direction of walking is likely to bring our epidermis into direct connection with the bark of a tree, and its bark is in this case just as bad as its bite. Especially if the tree is a dogwood.

This act of perceiving the tree involves in some way the act of automatically or habitually classifying the tree and possibly as that kind of obstacle to walking that we call a tree. We have made the practical equivalent of a general judgment, though we probably did not involve language in the process. We could involve language if we are questioned or if we are writing a book on the sense of humor.

Generally we perform these acts of classification without thinking, all day long and most of the night. But we can also consciously change the classification of the object. Sure, yon dogwood is a tree, but it can also be seen and classified as something else. We may automatically see it as a hazard to be avoided. We can also consciously see the tree in terms of a different set of interests or perspectives, or as a member of other classes of objects.

For example, the botanist sees it as a specific kind of tree, perhaps the Western Dogwood. An artist sees it as a unique pattern of lines and colors. The pest control salesman sees it as a source of revenue. The walker sees it as a source of pain because he spent too much time thinking about the tree and not enough time avoiding it. These things happen to people who think too much. Or too little.

The tree can thus be reclassified, re-understood, or reframed. We can see it differently. We can classify it differently. The general term under which it may be habitually classified is more or less consciously changed, and the object is seen or experienced in a new way.

So what does this have to do with a sense of humor? Will the questions never cease? Not for a philosopher. Or a nagging child.

A sense of humor is a playful appreciation of the incongruities in our lives. A sense of humor sees these incongruities in a new way, just as we can see the tree in a new way. A given incongruity may be an annoyance, or an object of apprehension, but it can also be a source of humor. And since the reclassification is done playfully, the result is often delight, pleasure, joy, or mirth.

For example, we may see an act of human stupidity. We can say something about the stupidity of the act, or about the character and perhaps the ancestry of the actor. On the other hand, we can put it in a larger context. We might try to see what the stupid act was most likely intended to produce. Or we might simply mutter, "What fools we mortals be." This may inspire reflection on the stupid things we ourselves have done. We might realize that the fool is supplying us with a great source of funny material. We ought to be grateful. Some of us are. Without our fools, our universe would be less rich. We do have a goodly supply of fools. Sometimes we find them in our mirror.

People are a great source of humorous material, and without people we would be a much spiritually poorer group. Some of us may find a reason for our existence in that observation.

To take a different example: A person we love dies. We can see this as a huge blow to our world. But we can also see it in the context of the universal human burden of making sense of it, and we have a new or at least a different perspective on this sad event. Sure, it still hurts, but we realize our loss is part of the pattern of life and death that is our heritage. We are to some extent, and perhaps to a large extent, able to deal with it in a different and more fruitful way. Not immediately, at first, in all likelihood, but sooner or later we realize we are just one being among many, that death is our end as it is for everyone. It may not make sense, but it at least fits into an understanding of our world.

We will have adopted a humorous appreciation for death, for example, when we remark, "Death is something one does not easily live through." Or "It's only the hope of dying that keeps me alive." At this point our sense of play is dealing with a major incongruity. We may have learned something important about our world and ourselves. We may have been able to deal with a potentially terrifying incongruity in a positive way. On the other hand, we may just be too sad to cry, and laughter is the only response we have left. People do occasionally laugh in the face of great tragedy. It is as expressive a gesture as any.

What goes on in the heart of a human being is often hard to access, even to the person himself. And that, my friend, is an incomprehensively philosophical remark. Or an incomprehensibly inane remark.

Getting to the later stages of realization may take a long time, and may never be achieved. But perhaps in a case like dealing with death, a sense of humor allows us to see another picture or context, a different and bigger picture or context, and reconcile us to our lives as mere mortals. Maybe not so "mere." Maybe as glorious mortals.

This example is extreme, but it illustrates how the ability to shift comparison classes, to reclassify a part of our world, may make a difference in the quality of our lives, even when it is done playfully. Perhaps especially because it is done playfully. It enables us to "roll with the punches," to understand to an extent the nature of our tragedy and of our lives. It does not diminish the loss. It may simply put it in a new, less self-oriented context. It can draw us out of our absorption in our own loss, of wallowing in our self-pity.

We might say, along with the philosopher Spinoza (1632-1677), that we are seeing our loss "under the aspect of eternity." I'm not going to say that because it seems excessively pretentious, but you can say it if you can keep a straight face.

Perhaps this is play made serous for a time, in order to help heal a wounded soul. Perhaps it is a skill that most happy people have, and most people who are not happy do not have. Perhaps this is part of the meaning of "flexibility." It may be the soul doing its equivalent of an aerobic workout. I just love silly metaphors.

Laughter by itself is rarely if ever able to give us new perspectives. The comedian may give us temporary relief from the pain and suffering in our world, or may make a good moment more enjoyable, but nothing more. We learn nothing from relief except the value of relief. And that's a relief. We don't have to learn great truths from everything.

What humor can do is no different from what great art can do, as I explore the analogy between the aesthetic and the humorous yet again. Of course there is a lot of what passes for art that is simply diversion, or entertainment. Pop art compares with comedy in our analogy. There is also a more profound kind of art, perhaps art properly so-called, or "fine art," which moves us strongly and involves us with some of the deeper questions of life. It helps us understand our world in some way, and perhaps to alter some of our perspectives. That is great or genuine art.

In the world of the funny, the equivalent of great art is humor. Telling great art from average or mediocre attempts at art may be difficult in many cases, at least at first. The same is true of trying to distinguish comedy from humor. It takes developed judgment or developed taste in both cases.

Can a person live effectively without a sense of humor? Some people seem to. Many of these people laugh occasionally. Many of the rewards of laughter can be won without any contact with humor. Comedy will serve quite well as playful distraction. Even the laughter that is part of most group identification behavior, or is functioning as a social lubricant, can distract. Nervous laughter can release some tension.

Humor tackles what comedy rarely does, which are the

serious incongruities, those involving ultimate questions of life, death, and our place in an incongruous universe. Humor allows us to deal with these incongruities in a way that is less serious, and perhaps less stark than these incongruities often seem to be. Humor invites us to explore anew our beliefs about these things. Can they be explored without humor? Certainly. But perhaps we often feel safer in dealing with them humorously rather than with the stark realization that we have no provable answers apart from the observation that we live and then we die, and we understand the latter even less than we understand the former.

Is the possession of a well-developed sense of humor a necessary condition for happiness? That's a very difficult problem, but tentatively I suggest that it is not. It is possible to be happy without a well-developed sense of humor. One can have many of the requisite attitudes and the skills to deal with problems, the flexibility and objectivity that seem to be important for happiness, and not have developed them as a consequence of the acquisition and exercise of a sense of humor.

But why bother to live without a sense of humor? I think a person can be happy without having or experiencing joy and delight, but it would be a rare person who could do this. Part of the quality of human existence would seem to never be attained by such a person. As far as I am concerned, a sense of humor is in almost all cases necessary for a happy life. Let those who are exceptions write their own book.

Conclusions

Long-term happiness seems to be superficially connected with laughter and comedy, but more essentially with a sense of humor. A sense of humor involves the ability to appreciate our lives and put our experiences into a different context, often a different comparison class, in a playful manner. This can also be called "reframing," or putting things in a different perspective. This ability is one of the characteristics of people who live happily in this world. Such an ability gives a more pleasant, often joyous sparkle to life. While laughter by itself does not indicate a great deal, and may occur in situations in which nothing is funny, and may even be an accompaniment to cruelty, a sense of humor usually avoids such situations. This suggests that a sense of humor needs to be controlled by a sense of morality, but that is beyond the scope of this chapter. We have enough problems as it is, conceptually speaking.

Endnotes

[1] I am intentionally not going to deal with the category of the hilarious. Every purported work of either comedy or humor is claimed by the advertisers to be "hilarious." I thought at first that a synonym for "hilarious" might be "side-splitting," but they are often used in the same sentence, and the writers of advertising copy surely cannot be guilty of redundancy. So I am going to instead deal with the category of the side-splitting, which seems to be a dangerous condition in which a person is injured, damaged, and probably in need of emergency medical service. How much of this carnage we can tolerate in an era of diminishing health services is debatable, but intentionally seeking a potentially maiming condition cannot be classified as either healthy or sane.[2]

[2] On the other hand, the "hysterical," often used to describe situations which might involve comedy, is a most useful condition in that it provides potential revenue for a galloping band of counselors, psychotherapist, and other mental health professionals who are bravely doing all they can to keep the inhabitants of this society somewhat sane. Good luck, guys.

"The humorless are the truly humorous."

Richard C. Richards

"Reality is a crutch for people who can't cope with drugs."

Lily Tomlin

"I've always been searching for a lifestyle that doesn't require my presence."

Richard "Kinky" Friedman

Chapter 8
Some Important Incongruities

There are certain questions that should to some extent be dealt with if genuine happiness is to be possible. These questions have to do with the meaning of existence, and of each individual human existence (especially our own). They include the challenges of forming good relationships with other people, the challenges of growing up, perhaps reproducing, and aging, the fact of death and what we can do about it (apart from simply dying), and the fret of our daily existence. This fret seems to be a part of our involvement with the practical details of living. This fret may involve the increasing amount of boredom in our contemporary lives, among other things. This fret also involves the increasingly excessive complexity of the details of our 21st century lives.[1]

A key problem: How does humor specifically help us deal with any of these issues?

A Magnificent Cop-Out

These are difficult questions, and I want to state a caveat regarding them. I have only tentative suggestions about how to think about these questions. I'm sorry to disappoint anyone looking for ultimate answers, but I am not in possession of much wisdom on these topics. I am striving at best for clarity and to suggest some lines of thinking regarding them, many of which involve the incongruities present in these questions.

You have to supply your own answers. I believe that if you have a sense of humor, your answers will satisfy you better than if you do not, partly because they are likely to have been carefully considered. Perhaps your answers have a better chance of being closer to the truth in some cases. We'll never know for sure.

One horrible truth I have saved until now, after you have bought the book and wasted a very small fraction of your life reading it. The horrible truth as I see it is that no one has ever had, presently has, or will ever have, knowledge that his answers to many of the very important questions are the truth. The best we can do is to have well-considered opinions or beliefs about the important questions. I am able to predict the future to this extent, but don't expect specifics on what will happen as time goes by. What time goes by I am not sure. Probably the present as it moves steadily toward the future. But you knew that.

Humorous Agnosticism

A sense of humor probably leads to a certain amount of agnosticism with regard to the certainty of many of one's opinions and beliefs, as well as those of other people. This often leads to a degree of tolerance with regard to the opinions of others. After all, if we cannot be certain with regard to the answers to many of the ultimate questions in life, it is silly to get heated up about it or to go to war over different answers to these questions. It may, however, be quite appropriate to go to war over other issues.

I am not saying that we should not take a stand on practical issues, especially moral ones. Stands should be taken, on the grounds of solid moral thinking and not because someone or some organization holds certain beliefs. But the possibility that we are wrong, or that we never know for sure, should add a bit of humility to our judgments. Moral issues often require commitment and action. We need enough honesty with regard to our own ability to make mistakes to carefully think and rethink moral issues, switching contexts to try to understand the issues better. To do less is not to be fully human.

Many ultimate issues, such as religious issues, are not essentially practical to the degree moral issues are, and therefore a great deal of tolerance is wise with regard to the answers other people give that may be different from our own. We can hope for the same degree of tolerance from other people, but we may not get it.[2]

Nevertheless you will most likely have come up with your own tentative answers to many of these questions in order to connect with your world and yourself. You can find plenty of ready-made answers to religious questions, but you might want to run them by the test of your own experience and those of other people.

These ultimate questions, whether religious or simply philosophical, often reflect on the incongruities of life and existence in general. If we are to be happy in this life, we most likely need to deal with some of the major incongruities. Will humor aid us in this task? I have suggested that it will.

It is time to say more about some major incongruities.

I mentioned previously that what is incongruous depends on the knowledge and expectations of the individual. This implies that what is incongruous to one person may not be incongruous to another, and what is incongruous to one person at one time may not be incongruous to the same person at another time. This is true of most incongruities, not only those that are playfully appreciated in humor.

While there are thousands if not millions of incongruities, some are more important, more cosmic, and more obvious than others. Some affect major portions of our lives, while some are hardly noticeable. Here are a few major paradoxes.

The Paradox of Life and Death

One common and potentially cosmic incongruity is the paradox of life, or perhaps it is better called the paradox of life and death. It is strange that something like life should end in death, that life and death are occurring simultaneously all around us, and that from dead things new life emerges. Human life, which is the most important form of life for us, seems to end in its opposite. A person who was living is no longer living, though the corpse is still a source of economic exploitation.

The death of natural objects involved with autumn produces new life in the spring. Who is in charge of this stuff, anyway?

The fortunate person learns the joys of living and thriving, of growing and developing, and then is sooner or later confronted by the reality of diminishing powers and death, if the normal cycle of growth and decay is not interrupted. That which grows and thrives also declines and dies. It is true of all living things, the child discovers. The status quo is soon gone, quo-ing no more. The status which quos at dawn does not quo by evening, and this truth comes home to roost.

This situation is particularly hard to understand. Those we love die sooner or later, and we find the signs of death showing up in our own bodies in the form of lines and wrinkles, sags and creases, aches and pains, and diminished physical and mental capacities. Physiologists tell us that we've pretty much peaked out in most areas before we reach the age of twenty, but of course the road downhill is slow in most cases. Many of us try to make it even slower. Some of us try to stop it entirely.

I don't know if we human beings are the only animals that know we will die, but perhaps we are the only animals that can see it as a tragedy. First the ones we love, and then we ourselves, will have our cliché conversation with the Grim Reaper. It doesn't seem to matter what we say. Perhaps at that point all speech is a cliché.

The American philosopher Herbert Fingarette (1921 -present) has put this paradox most clearly: "It's a strange, perplexing world where love is the proof that life can be shared, death is the proof that it can't."[3]

Death doesn't fit. It's absurd. It's a reality.

Faced with this reality, the mind often shows a capacity for denial. We may hope that the belief that life ends in death, and death is the end, simply is not true, despite the physical evidence of inert corpses suggesting physical life is over. It is so incompatible with what we feel and need. We hope that consciousness can continue without the physical body, though we have never seen any clear example of it in our physical lives.

Religions most likely appeared about the same time as complex conceptual thought, and attempted to resolve the incongruity of life and death, to right the wrong, to make sense of it all. I am not saying that religion is true or false. Religion is a way to make sense of death, feeding on the human need for understanding and reconciliation. Or simply to avoid the terror of the thought of our possible physical non-existence. What a loss that would be to the world! One can hardly imagine it.

While some people claim that death is much too serious a topic to be treated humorously, that has not deterred the humorists. The following are examples of the humorous treatment of death. I have been unable to trace the authors of these comments.

"Death is nature's way of telling you to slow down."

"Death is something one does not easily live through."

"It is only the hope of dying that keeps me alive."

"The meaning of life is that it stops."

The Meaning of Life

Another important question is whether life in general, or our life in particular, has any meaning. Why are we here? What should we be doing? Is life, as one Brit claimed, only the tale of an idiot, full of sound and fury, but signifying nothing?

This question is complicated further when we realize that what seems important to us (the fret of our own existence, our little problems and passions, and the goals we strive for) will mean almost nothing to people a hundred years from now. We will all be gone, at least physically, or if one of us is not, he just may wish he were gone. The frets of people a hundred years ago are mostly unknown, or if known, are sometimes interesting when we look at the preserved accounts. They certainly give us one perspective from which to view our own little dramas.

Perhaps we each have to find our own meaning for our lives if we are to be honest and not accept the ready-made meanings that society gives us to help us avoid the terror of existence—or non-existence. The meaning of our existence seems temporary, and temporal, when we view the scope of human history. Perhaps we can construct an over-riding theme or meaning, but since different people construct different meanings, it leaves an honest person with a touch of philosophical indigestion, the result of biting off a little more metaphysics than he can chew.

The meaning of life remains an open question for someone who does not demand fast answers at the expense of truth. The meaning of any individual's life seems to be made up of that person's thoughts and actions while they are alive. In the long run that may be all there is.

The Specific Paradoxes of Religion

Now enter some other important paradoxes, stage right, and when viewed playfully, are rich sources for humor. You can call this set of paradoxes "religion, or a quest for the divine." There may be a divine source for our universe, but religious philosophies, which usually attempt to explain the origins of everything, are man-created entities, and as such are subject to all the human frailties and foibles to which human philosophies are prone. The fact that religions often disagree with each other makes the question more complex...or more humorous. "What fools we mortals be."

Even if we receive the entire truth about these issues directly from a divine being in position to know, it is hard to imagine that we could understand it or convey it clearly and accurately to others. Or not disagree over what was in fact said by the divine source or what the words we received mean.

Of course all of these considerations involve incongruities. The fun starts. Most religions claim to be the true one, the one instituted and supported by God, gods, the Cosmic Muffin, or whatever principle they want, and by whatever name they wish to call it or them. Since most religions claim to be the true one, we have the immediate incongruity of their disagreement.

I am going to draw some specific examples of the incongruities of specific religions from the Judeo-Christian tradition, since that is the one I know the most about. This tradition claims that God is love, but the participants may engage in hateful activities such as torturing and killing those who don't agree.[4]

The various sects within the Christian traditions may even claim that God ordered the slaughter of innocents. I have in mind here some activities of Christianity, such as the Crusades, though contemporary conservative Christians can still pick off an abortion doctor or two when the opportunity arises, just to keep the tradition alive and well. Conversion in the name of a religion based on "love" has often been bloody indeed. Needless to say other major religions could be cited on this score and the incongruities they harbor are ripe for enjoyment by the humorist, though not necessarily by the believers.

Christianity is full of intellectual incongruities, as pointed out by Soren Kierkegaard (1813-1855), a Danish Christian theologian. For instance, the infinite becomes finite, spirit becomes flesh, the divine becomes human and yet perfect, a virgin becomes pregnant. I could go on and on, and I am not particularly trying to pick on Christianity. Other traditions have their own paradoxes to deal with. Only those mystics who refuse to speak on the issues may avoid the puzzles. However, many mystics claim they are simultaneously in space and time and beyond space and time when they have their mystical experiences of the ultimate. This qualifies as a pretty good incongruity in its own right.

Do cell phones work beyond time and space? What is the area code of the timeless? If you get an answer on your cosmic cell, and the wrong deity answers, do you just hang up? Or politely say you dialed the wrong number and quickly forget about it?[5]

There are more incongruities. One theory is that after our physical life is over, we go to a place called heaven. One version of this belief is that we will have immaterial bodies, which is an interesting incongruity in itself. In one version of heaven we will spend an infinite amount of time playing harps, an instrument which many of us find limited, monotonous, and even tedious, in this life. The pleasures of the physical body will be long gone. We will not suffer from terminal boredom since there will be no way to end the endless succession of boring experiences. Eternal boredom is perhaps supposed to be self-justifying.

Or we will praise some god or other. Forever. Why this god needs or allows this praise is not clear. Perfect beings normally do not need a boost to their self-esteem. The value of such behavior for our own psychological development isn't clear either. It appears offhand to be pretty juvenile.

One more wonderful incongruity before we move on. God or some cosmic principle is introduced to explain where the whole universe came from. Everything, after all, has a cause. God caused the universe.

If everything has a cause, then it is logical to ask for the cause of God. But, it is claimed, God does not have a cause. The explanation for this is that God is self-caused. Now if the cause precedes the effect, then God preceded himself.[6]

Or it may be claimed that God is uncaused, an exception to the principle of causation. How convenient. How paradoxical. How incongruous. Perhaps it is so, but the claim is not reasonable.

Nor am I willing to let the theoretical physicists off the hook. They deal with generalities that are unimaginable to the human mind. It takes quality cartooning to hide this fact. The Big Bang defies understanding, and the various changes in this theory follow one another with regularity, none of them particularly explaining where it all came from, if it came from everything or anywhere. The problem remains: Why is there something rather than nothing? I'm not sure we even understand the question, but I often know an incongruity when I see one. I'll bet you do too.

The Paradoxes of Being Human

The human being is a bundle of incongruities. With conflicting desires, high intentions and less than high actions, with a body that thrives and languishes, grows and decays, is born young and grows old, we paddle on the pond of life, waiting for or not thinking about the ultimate shipwreck that awaits us. We're a self-centered speck in the cosmos. We often think our own values are the right and perhaps ultimate values, even with the knowledge that other people and other cultures have different and often equally successful ways of dealing with life's little problems. We see a vast array of often incompatible religious beliefs. We know that there is more than one way to skin a cat, but we don't know what to do with skinned cats.[7]

Is it time to take the clichés out of the bag and put them with the incongruities on the table?

We come in two varieties, male and female, just similar enough to lull us into a false sense that we are really alike, and that understanding each other is easy. It takes both of us to create a new human life, and this is done in an essentially humorous way. We unite parts of our bodies that are very clumsy to unite. Then that one new life we create turns our previous lives upside down. And we now have yet another life trying to make sense of it all, hopefully with some parental help. Or hindrance. For this purpose, each child should try to have some parents of its own.

Parenthood offers some nice incongruities. We swear we will not impart to our children the hang-ups we possess as a heritage from our own parents, and yet we often do inflict those hang-ups. We ignore the fact that bringing up a human being is necessarily to warp that human being in some way or another, and such warping is a parent's job. One hopes for a fortuitous warp or two. Our job as a person is to discover the warp in the wood we were given by our parents and do some carpenter work. Being a chip off the old block has some disadvantages.

To use a religious image, we are half angel and half devil, and sometimes it is hard to tell which part is which. In the name of love and respect we do things that are unloving and disrespectful. How's that for an incongruity? Is it any better to be half human and half goat, as the ancient Greeks suggested? The image of the satyr suggests the ancient Greeks considered this image might be a better image for trying to understand the bundle of incongruities that is the human being.

We know that the effect of words can hurt, but the pain words cause can usually be overcome. Yet we attempt to ban certain words, just making them more powerful. How's that for a paradox? Have you used the "N word" recently? Why not? It has a tremendous range of meaning if we would just look at it objectively, and we can learn a lot from it.

That's just a start with regard to the collection of incongruities that is the human being. You can continue the listing. Or ask a humorist to do it.

Dealing with Incongruity

There are various ways to deal with an incongruity. One way is to ignore it, on the perhaps mistaken grounds that it is not important in the scheme of things. Perhaps it is not. The incongruity between hot and cold is usually not important unless there is too much of either. A humorist might make something of this, but you and I usually don't.

Another way to deal with incongruities is to become frightened. We see the reality of death and it is not pleasant. One way to deal with an incongruity is to deny it. Death is just "the other side of life." That's an old advertising slogan. Now, don't you feel better? Lots of dead people do.

Some incongruities upset us in other ways. The incongruity between wealth and poverty, plenty and little, the haves and the have-nots, has started more than one reformer on the path toward social justice, often without asking what the consequences of social justice would be. Rage can be a pretty strong motivator.

Perhaps some incongruities just have to be accepted. The incongruity of a healthy person being stretched out in the operating room because of a sudden accident or the discovery of a tumor can cause fear, anger, and disappointment. But there is little we can do at this point. We are helpless, and our trust is in the medical team that will be exploring our personal space with some fearsome looking instruments, with no guarantee of success. The situation is sometimes hopeless, but not serious, as one patient put it somewhat humorously.[8]

Humor can help deal with all these situations, often by putting the incongruity in another perspective or comparing the situation with one we might not normally bring in. If you can see the incongruity playfully and find a way to laugh at it, to see its funny implications, you are not stuck in a position of being unable to do something. You can at least joke. By doing that, you can take a step to avoid the depressing situation of being helpless. Plus, that which is the object of humor can become more familiar, and the familiar is often less threatening.

Conclusion

To sum it up, I have investigated some of the major incongruities with which people have been occupied for quite a while. Life, religions, and we ourselves are full of paradoxes and incongruities. After such a thorough examination, we don't have to be involved with incongruities anymore. Or maybe we do.

Endnotes

[1] That's plenty to be concerned about.

[2] This incongruity is not particularly humorous.

[3] Fingarette, Herbert. *Death: Philosophical Soundings.* Chicago: Open Court, 1995. Look Ma. An actual footnote.

[4] "Thor speaking. Whom do you wish thunder-bolted today. We're having a special on Druids."

[5] What does your GPS tell you when you're beyond space and time? "Recalculating...recalculating...oh crap"?

[6] How do you do cause yourself? Simple. Use an alias.

[7] Or skinned clichés.

[8] "Not a shred of evidence exists in favor of the idea that life is serious." *Brendan Gill*

Chapter 8: Some Important Incongruities

*"Our national drug is alcohol. We tend
to regard the use of any other drug with
special horror."*
> William S. Burroughs

*"What I look forward to is continued
immaturity followed by death."*
> Dave Barry

"Never take a whiz on an electric fence."

> Richard "Kinky" Friedman

Chapter 9
Loose Ends

Congrats!

You're the first person to read these words. I quit reading long ago because it was too complex and boring. While we're here, we might as well deal with some of the questions that have been hanging around on the sidelines. No doubt you've been saving them for now.

A Question

Do we really need a distinction between comedy and humor?

We need this distinction because we're trying to understand a part of our world and ourselves. That is one of the philosopher's missions in life, and was recommended by no less authority than the Greek philosopher, Aristotle himself. You know the guy. He was converted to Christianity in the 13th century by a radical alteration to almost every philosophical position he held.

The distinction is useful if you want to understand what is going on when people laugh, especially with regard to the things that make them laugh. Ultimately we'll all be dead in a century or two, and maybe people then will still think it useful to pursue these questions. But right now it could help us understand a bit better. It might even give us some tools to deal with our world. Let those who come after us do their own philosophizing. They'll probably insist on it.

For one thing, the distinction helps us distinguish between humorists, who are artists in their own right, and comedians, who are merely trying to make a buck or two. Comedians will get a laugh in any way possible, including dropping their pants, and if they get any notoriety at all, it is often because they perform their function well. Humorists, on the other hand, give us insight and tend to be appreciated in their lives and afterwards. The same distinction can be found between house painters and great painters. House painters may be skilled craftsmen, but their freshly painted structures are rarely the object of guided tours. Salvador Dali, on the other hand, is remembered, and I doubt he painted many houses.

There is a difference between Ricky Thomason and George Carlin. Who, you ask, is Ricky Tomason? You just made my point. It's as if he had never existed.

Of course the distinction between comedy and humor is not airtight. Any funny man can range from comedy (the search for laughter in an audience) to humor (the playful exploration of incongruities), and it may be hard to immediately tell which is which at any given time. But the discussion may help us understand the function of comedy and humor in human life, and perhaps suggest more effective ways to live.

Few categories are airtight. The category of blue, to use our earlier example, is not airtight in the sense that it runs into green on one side, violet on the other, and other colors from time to time. Sometimes it is hard to know what word to use to describe a color that is nearly blue.

Another, Related Question

Isn't this distinction between comedy and humor just another attempt to make word usage clear, and, like most such attempts, will be honored by being completely ignored?

Right. Most people will not know about this distinction, and if they knew, they would not follow the suggestion of regarding the two as separate in theory, though often not in practice. It is not useful for them. I hope it is useful for people who are concerned with understanding the issues. This would include psychologists and other social scientists whose research efforts occasionally suffer from an inability to distinguish comedy and its goal from humor and its goal. They study laughter, and think they are studying humor. They study behavior, and think they can use it to accurately interpret what is going on in the mind.

The goal of the social scientists is often to quantify observable behavior, which for their and our purposes is laughter. People laugh at various things for various reasons. Laughter, no matter how raucous or prolonged, is not a sign of humor, or even of what is funny. If we have not established that by now, I will state it one last time. To try to measure a sense of humor or other similar human characteristic by means of the laughter produced by a possible funny object is like trying to measure the degree of sexual excitement present by measuring skin temperature. Or to measure the degree of honesty of a politician by whether his eyes are lower than or higher than his ears. Too many other factors are involved.

If you are still asking the question of whether the issue is one of terminological clarity, the answer is yes. I am recommending more careful term usage for the sake of clarity of understanding. I do not expect to have much impact on the average person's term usage, nor do I particularly want to. Verbal habits are hard to modify.

Most people don't need the degree of clarity that such a modification would produce. For them laughter is self-justifying and they identify laughter with humor.

Still Another Question

If laughter is important in any way for human beings, what does its source matter?

No doubt laughter is important for several reasons, which I intended to establish in this book. But what is going on in the mind while laughter lingers around the lips is supremely important. It seems to me that humor aims at insight, which is not the goal of comedy. Distraction from problems and the regeneration of energy which laughter can accomplish is good, but insight into ourselves and our world, which humor can produce, is even better. If this is so, then understanding what we expect from laughter is important. Humor has more implications for our ultimate happiness, and we ought to seek it more often.

Analogously, it may be better to seek out a performance of Beethoven's Ninth than to content ourselves with whistling "Twinkle, Twinkle Little Star." But you expected I would revert to that analogy again. I am happy not to disappoint you.

Let's tackle another analogy. Think of the laughter generated by the violent antics of *The Three Stooges*. Their laughter-provoking capers involve punching, hitting, tweaking, poking and in general assaulting the body of one another. What insight does that provide? I cringe, but call it an example of comedy: Relief-theory comedy. There are probably a few people in our world we would like to punch, hit, tweak, poke, or otherwise assault, but we dare not because of the consequences.

On the other hand, exploring the incongruity between cruelty and laughter can lead to some interesting and informative trains of thought. The same can be said of our inclination to laugh at the pain or misfortune of others.

Compare this to some of the monologues of the late George Carlin, who explored the characteristics of our culture and ourselves in ways that often provokes laughter, and provide us with the opportunity to gain some understanding of ourselves by exploring the paradoxes that we human beings present.

Yet Another Question

Let's examine again my contention of the relationship between humor and the aesthetic world. Is there any relationship there at all?

It seems to me there is, and I could cite others who agree, and from whom I learned this relationship. But rather than appeal to authority, which often becomes a question of who can produce the most believable, or famous authority, I throw it to the ultimate authority, which is that of the reader. Does it seem, based on your experience of what I have called humor, that humor shares many characteristics with aesthetic experience?

I've made my case on this point. I can now only ask for some honest introspection. I hope you have thought about these issues as you have read the book, and that your range of experience allows you to make this observation on ample grounds.

A Significant Question

There you go again, you author you. You're maintaining that some people's introspection is better than other people's introspection. You are introducing the issue of good taste again, aren't you?

Yes.

A Revealing Question

Does good taste imply that a person agrees with your introspection?

I hope so. I've worked and played for years to understand my world. I've tried to participate in my world as fully as I can. I've found the expressive power of art in its many forms. I've dabbled a bit with that expressive power myself. I've pursued humor with a sometimes humorless intensity. I've found many people who said things so clearly for me that I could not help but see the truth of what they pointed out. I am grateful for having spent time with them.

I am grateful for all the people who have thought about these issues. I've used my own experience as the ultimate test. I recommend that you use yours in a like manner if you don't already. If we agree, it is a little scary in that I am not challenged by agreement and may stop thinking for a while. If we do not agree, then I can learn from you. And I learn more about me, if I really want that particular kind of knowledge.

But you're probably wrong if we disagree in any major way and cannot talk it though.

Do you expect me to deny my own experience? Do you expect me to take your word for it? I will if it fits my experience as I have come to understand it. You may help me understand it. I may help you understand your experience. But ultimately if we disagree, I can only say that our experiences have perhaps been quite different, or one of us has not understood his experience very well. Perhaps we are both wrong.

Words are mysterious, strange things. Mystical silence has its value.

Jokes and Humor

Please recall for the sake of clarity that I have stipulated that the adjective "funny" can be used to denote anything capable of producing laughter of any kind. "Funny peculiar" deals with laughter of a nervous or frightened nature. So laughing does not necessarily indicate that anything comical or humorous is going on.

Jokes involved with the production of social adhesion seldom involve anything humorous, but they can.

Joking usually has little to do with humor. A joke, if effective, may tap into a prejudice, release some tension (thanks, Sigmund), make us more comfortable, or do other things. It has many social purposes, most of them quite benign. Humor, on the other hand, shows a developmental quality, with parts building on parts, until hopefully some insight is gained. Jokes can be humorous, but they are not automatically so.

Jokes seek laughs, for whatever purposes. Humor seeks insights. Jokes often, but not always, work on the basis of surprise. There is usually a sudden shift in consciousness, which is pleasurable in some way or other. Jokes are almost always relatively brief, with the exception of practical jokes, which may be elaborate, but are still based on surprise. Shaggy dog stories violate the rule that a verbal joke is usually short. By contrast, there can be humor without surprise. Good jokes reward retelling, a characteristic they share with much humor. I called this the "persistence of humor" earlier in the book. I still call it that now.

The above paragraph is a potential quote source for someone who is assigned the task of summarizing some of the conclusions of this book. If you underline as a habit, please underline this in red, white, and blue. The white won't show up. It's the thought that counts.

Why Not Another Question?

How prevalent is a sense of humor in the population of most western cultures? A well-developed sense of humor is not common enough. There is, of course, considerable laughter, but laughter has no one-to-one correlation with the presence of humor, as I pointed out monotonously several times earlier. Believing as I do that a sense of humor is at the very least similar to a sense of the aesthetic, and believing that a well-developed sense of the aesthetic is not very common, I see no other conclusion to draw, though it would delight me to learn that everyone has a highly developed sense of both. Evidence does not support that claim.

Unfortunately I do not see that our economically oriented culture, western culture, places much value on developing either a sense of the aesthetic or a sense of humor. That the arts are as well supported as they are, is a source of wonder and delight to me. I understand in our culture that art has partially become an economic token, which has nothing to do with aesthetic value.

It is obvious that laughter is fairly highly valued in our culture, given its non-economic benefits. Laughter supplies relief and distraction from the serious business of making money. Laughter can bind us together. But humor? To the extent that humor can provoke laughter, or a humorist can use incongruity to build a sense of delight and often of laughter, the humorist can succeed popularly and economically. Economic success decreases the chances of starving to death, which is not very humorous.

Humorists are also a pain in the (choose your body part) because they tend to question too many things, many of which are nearly sacred cows. They might even make fun of the sacred ones if they are in the mooood.

So Who are the Humorists?

You are asking for examples of humorists? Past humorists such as Mark Twain and Will Rogers did pretty well in earning enough money, eventually, to practice their humor on a fairly large scale. In the contemporary world Dave Barry has done well over a considerable period of time, especially since he knows how to bring out the funny characteristics of his material and often produces laughs when his material is read. Written humor is perhaps the hardest to create. The British team, Monty Python, did some humorous work, but developed a split personality. Jon Stewart, Stephen Colbert, and Bill Maher have taken political and social commentary into the realm of humor on occasion. The late George Carlin was good at it.

There are no doubt many others, but the above serve

as examples since they are fairly well known. I have not singled them out because they get laughs, but because they playfully discover, often create, and exploit incongruity on occasion. But they do other things to get laughs, which help them to have yet another year or two in the public eye. Keeping the proverbial wolf away from the proverbial door is good, proverbially speaking.

Most of these humorists cited are on the political left. That causes me to examine the political right, but apart from an occasional piece of humor by Rush Limbaugh, the right seems to be a relatively humorless place. There are plenty of funny character assassinations, and fixedly determined efforts to laugh at the political left, but I do not find much humor on the political right.

Lest I be charged with bias, I would have to report that the radical left seems to be a relatively humorless place also, apart from its humorists. The competition for the least humorous political position between the extreme left and the extreme right is a true clash of the titans.

So You're a Damned Elitist, Aren't You?

I suppose so, if you want to use that label, though I think I am reporting what I have learned in what I hope is a fairly clear way. I don't see much sign of a well-developed sense of humor in most people. They can laugh easily in many cases, but their appreciation for incongruity is pretty weak. They laugh mostly at the things they are supposed to laugh at, such as politicians and the opposite sex. They are usually social laughers, and they are often fun to be around. Insight from laughter is not their goal, and probably not their accomplishment in most cases. Relief and ridicule seem to be the main items on their menu. They often attain the various values produced by the various kinds of laughter. They seldom get any insight from whatever makes them laugh. Humor is not common for them.

So is this elitist? Few people are good enough at basketball to play it professionally. Are those people who can play it professionally elitist? You tell me. Or are they just realists when it comes to evaluating the basketball abilities or potential abilities of most of the population? The question is not a slam-dunk, but it is an interesting one.

Should we expect a well-developed sense of humor to be any more distributed in the population than a well-developed sense of the aesthetic? There seems to be a weak sense of the aesthetic in many if not all people, but a well-developed sense of the aesthetic takes effort and time. The same is true of a well-developed sense of humor. People like to laugh, and the cultural pattern seems to be that men are expected to make women laugh. Hopefully a man does it with cleverness and grace, but contemporarily in the media it often seems that men are the cause of laughter simply by their ineffectiveness as people, workers, or as fathers or grandfathers. No doubt someone will soon see the humorous aspects of that shift in the laughableness of men if someone has not seen it already, and exploit the real humor of this incongruity. We seem to expect men to be strong, well intentioned, but ineffective. Hearts of oak and heads to match.

Conclusion

I suppose I ought to conclude with a sweeping view of the future of humor, comedy, and even laughter. It is a hopeful future if we can keep laughter, comedy, and especially humor. It would be a real help if the quality of comedy could be elevated, but as it has been observed, in paraphrase: No one was ever guilty of underestimating the sense of humor of the American public. In this age of laugh tracks, laughter is cheap and sometimes meaningless. Contact laughter is the last refuge of a scoundrel.

Probably people will continue laughing, comedy will flourish to keep us from realizing just how bad things are or might get, and hopefully humor will not only help us get through it, but maybe even show the way on occasion. Comedy and humor will continue to add sparkle to our existence, lest our lives become an open can of day-old cola. One can hope for such a future. If the worst happens, and the human race is no more, we will have lost our biggest source of humorous material. We'll no doubt be the worse for it.

"I'm writing a book. I've got the page numbers done."

Stephen Wright

Afterword

I am not the first and will not be the last to acknowledge the amount of labor involved in thinking through and writing a book. There is often a partner in life who sustains and supports the effort in so many ways. For me it is my wife Marlene, who also brings considerable critical skills to the job of editing. You can judge by now that I sorely need these skills, and probably haven't taken advantage of her suggestions to the extent I might. As it is, without her judgment this book would have been twice as long, four times as boring, and much less clear.

I won't name most of the people who have influenced, helped, guided, challenged, and in general have been my intellectual stimulants. Herbert Fingarette inspired me to become a philosopher. Many people furthered that process. I want to especially mention The Lighthearted Philosophers' Society, whose annual meetings have provided me richly with the realization I did not understand numerous issues very well, and probably still don't. Dave Monroe, the spiritual leader of this band, deserves special thanks. So do other colleagues who have shown interest, talked about the issues, provided encouragement, and in some cases read chapters of the book, which is quite beyond the call of duty. Or sanity.

Special thanks and gratitude to publisher Katharina Notarianni, whose unfailing good humor, good taste in design questions, and general encouragement and competence made the process of publication one of appreciation rather an apprehension.

Trying to ride the twin horses of serious philosophy of laughter and humor on the one side, and the production of humor on the other side, may have divided my psyche into two incongruous and irreconcilable elements.

No big problem.

I have tried to avoid the plague of professional and usually obscure terminology, sticking instead to ordinary terms I have tried by stipulation to make more precise. I have even more intentionally avoided references to physiological phenomena since the use of terminology involving these is subject to the vicissitudes of progress and whim. New fads emerge with regularity.

For instance I could have explored the physiological concomitant states of the brain when laughter or the enjoyment of humor is going on. That connection is similar to the action of the pistons in the motor of a car and its connection with the sensation of skillfully navigating a corner at speed and experiencing the thrill of competence and accomplishment that fast cornering can bring.

In other words I don't care what is going on in the brain, and I fail to see any relevance to the understanding of laughter and humor. I know such accounts are contemporarily popular. I don't care at all if there is excitation in the pre-agonistic cortex subject to secretions from the quasiepidural gland. The quasiepidural gland doesn't care either.

For me philosophy has always been a highly personal activity, and I wanted to write a book that mirrored that. I hope I have succeeded.

I wish this book, or something like it, would have been available to me as a graduate student in philosophy. We needed a book in which the joy of doing philosophy was combined with the attempt to do some philosophy.

Philosophers and others in the liberal arts and social sciences have been scared to death by the progress and results attained by the hard sciences, and have often attempted to emulate the sparse, analytic, and obscure style of those scientific writings. Perhaps they hope to gain some respectability thereby. There is, of course, a place for careful scholarship in any serious discipline, even if it can become excessively obscure for the average person. It is, however, not the be all and end all of careful thinking. Careful thinking about nothing produces nothing.

The quality of such works is all too often judged by the number of footnotes and range of citations. Citing certain famous and approved authors is also very important. Those are interesting and quaint criteria. This is also why, in this book, there are few footnotes, no index, and only a limited table of contents.

One person described philosophy as the systematic abuse of an elaborate technical vocabulary invented specifically for that purpose. This description magnificently describes the serious works of many of the professional articles and books in philosophy as well as those of the sciences, both social and hard

There is also a place for lightening up, for avoiding technical language and the often-accompanying obscurity. W. H. Auden suggested that at some point whole epics would be written in private languages. That has been true for centuries. It is not the only alternative.

Combining a light touch with some heavy thinking is not

easy. It requires some heavy lifting. That does not mean we should not try.

A Philosopher Looks at The Sense of Humor

About The Author

Richard C. Richards, Professor of Philosophy Emeritus, taught various philosophy courses at California State Polytechnic University, Pomona, for nearly forty odd years.

Actually only half those years were odd. The other half were even. It is odd that even the even years were a bit odd. And the odd years were surprisingly even, though there were odd moments.

He taught courses in Philosophy of the Arts, Ancient Philosophy, Medieval Philosophy, Logic and Semantics, Ethics, Business and Professional Ethics, Philosophy of Love and Sex, Aristotle, Existentialism, and The Philosophy of Humor.

He earned his undergraduate degree at the University of California Santa Barbara, and his graduate degrees at UCLA, where he specialized in medieval philosophy, especially the philosophies of William Ockham and John of Mirecourt.

Richard and his wife of thirty years, Marlene, are enjoying retirement with travel, operas, and concerts. He also hybridizes irises and has won national awards with his introductions of irises into the national iris trade.

Visit Richard Richards on the web at

www.PhilosopherLooksAtHumor.com

www.ingramcontent.com/pod-product-compliance
Lightning Source LLC
Chambersburg PA
CBHW070806100426

42742CB00012B/2270